CAMPAIGN • 205

WARSAW 1944

Poland's bid for freedom

ROBERT FORCZYK ILLUSTRATED BY PETER DENNIS

Series editors Marcus Cowper and Nikolai Bogdanovic

First published in Great Britain in 2009 by Osprey Publishing,
Midland House, West Way, Botley, Oxford OX2 0PH, UK
44-02 23rd St, Suite 219, Long Island City, NY 11101, USA
E-mail: info@ospreypublishing.com

© 2009 Osprey Publishing Ltd

Print ISBN: 978 1 84603 352 0
PDF e-book ISBN: 978 1 84603 869 3

Editorial by Ilios Publishing Ltd, Oxford, UK (www.iliospublishing.com)
Page layout by The Black Spot
Index by Alison Worthington
Typeset in Sabon and Myriad Pro
Maps by Bounford.com
3D bird's-eye views by The Black Spot
Battlescene illustrations by Peter Dennis
Originated by PDQ Digital Media Solutions
Printed in China through Worldprint Ltd.

10 11 12 13 14   11 10 9 8 7 6 5 4 3 2

FOR A CATALOGUE OF ALL BOOKS PUBLISHED BY OSPREY MILITARY
AND AVIATION PLEASE CONTACT:

Osprey Direct, c/o Random House Distribution Center,
400 Hahn Road, Westminster, MD 21157
E-mail: uscustomerservice@ospreypublishing.com

Osprey Direct, The Book Service Ltd, Distribution Centre,
Colchester Road, Frating Green, Colchester, Essex, CO7 7DW
E-mail: customerservice@ospreypublishing.com

www.ospreypublishing.com

ACKNOWLEDGEMENTS

I would like to thank Monika Geilen at the Bundesarchiv, Joanna
Jastrzebska at the Warsaw Uprising Museum, Michelle at HITM Archives
and Nik Cornish for providing help with locating photographs. I would also
like to thank Steven Zaloga for his insights on the Polish resistance and
gracious loan of research materials.

DEDICATION

This volume is dedicated to the memory of Generał brygady Stefan Paweł
Rowecki (1895–1944), a true son of Poland.

ARTIST'S NOTE

Readers may care to note that the original paintings from which the
colour plates in this book were prepared are available for private sale.
All reproduction copyright whatsoever is retained by the Publishers.
All enquiries should be addressed to:

Peter Dennis, Fieldhead, The Park, Mansfield, Notts, NG18 2AT, UK

The Publishers regret that they can enter into no correspondence upon
this matter.

THE WOODLAND TRUST

Osprey Publishing are supporting the Woodland Trust, the UK's leading
woodland conservation charity, by funding the dedication of trees.

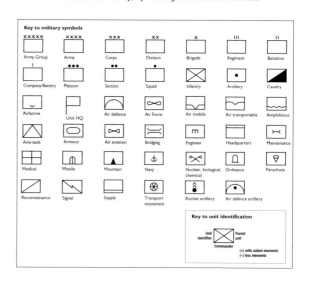

COMPARATIVE OFFICER RANKS

British Army	German Army	Waffen-SS	Polish Army
Second Lieutenant	Leutnant	Untersturmführer	Podporucznik
First Lieutenant	Oberleutnant	Obersturmführer	Porucznik
Captain	Hauptmann	Hauptsturmführer	Kapitan
Major	Major	Sturmbannführer	Major
Lieutenant-Colonel	Oberstleutnant	Obersturmbannführer	Podpulkownik
Colonel	Oberst	Standartenführer	Pulkownik
Brigadier	Generalmajor	Oberführer/Brigadeführer	
Major-General	Generalleutnant	Gruppenführer	General brygady
Lieutenant-General	General	Obergruppenführer	General dywizji
General	Generaloberst	Oberstgruppenführer	General broni
Field Marshal	Generalfeldmarschall	Reichsführer-SS	Marszalek

CONTENTS

ORIGINS OF THE CAMPAIGN

Poland's existence is intolerable and incompatible with the essential conditions of Germany's life.
Generaloberst Hans van Seeckt, 1922

After more than a century of German and Russian occupation, Poland once again became an independent state at the end of World War I. However, Poland's new-found liberty was precarious from the start and its leader, Jozef Pilsudski, had to fend off a Soviet invasion that reached the approaches to Warsaw in 1920. While Pilsudski succeeded in defeating this aggression, he decided to base Poland's long-term security upon a defensive military alliance with France and non-aggression treaties with Germany and the Soviet Union. Poland signed a formal military alliance with France in 1921, which provided defensive guarantees against both Germany and the Soviet Union. In 1932, the Soviet Union finally signed a non-aggression pact with Poland and Hitler signed a 10-year non-aggression pact with Poland in 1934. Although Pilsudski seemed to have stabilized Poland's security situation, his increasing perception of the four main opposition parties as internal security threats took the gloss off the Polish national unity acquired in 1918. After Pilsudski's death in 1935, his disciples established the Sanacja ('cleansing') regime – essentially a quasi-military dictatorship – that succeeded in alienating much of the population. Just as Poland was descending into a period of internal rancour, the threat of foreign aggression re-emerged as Nazi Germany re-armed and began to push an aggressive agenda in Eastern Europe. After the 1938 Munich Crisis, Poland's leaders sought new guarantees from both the West and from Stalin. For the first time, Poland sought and received a British security commitment in March 1939, followed by French guarantees of military support in May 1939. Stalin continued to re-affirm the Soviet–Polish non-aggression pact even as he was negotiating with Hitler to carve up Poland.

GERMAN AND SOVIET OCCUPATION, 1939–41

We have already formed displacement policies regarding the Polish population within Poland; the ultimate task is to wipe out the Poles and repopulate lands that rightfully belong to Germany.
Adolf Hitler, 13 April 1941

Indeed, of all the foreign leaders with whom Poland had to contend, Hitler was probably the most honest, in that his hatred was undisguised. Hitler abrogated the 1934 non-aggression pact in April 1939 and, using the sensitive issue of Danzig as an excuse, actively began preparing for invasion. Hitler also had a better sense than Poland's leaders that Anglo-French security guarantees were worthless. Putting aside Nazi–Soviet political differences

OPPOSITE
Germany and the Soviet Union were equally guilty in the destruction of the Polish Republic. Here, Soviet tank brigade commander Semyon Krivoshein hosts a joint German–Soviet victory parade with General der Panzertruppen Heinz Guderian in Brest-Litovsk on 22 September 1939. (AKG Images, 74575)

5

for the moment, Hitler authorized the Molotov–Ribbentrop Pact, signed on 23 August 1939. In the secret protocol to the pact, Hitler and Stalin agreed to divide up Poland between them, with Warsaw going to the German zone. Nine days later, Germany invaded Poland. Hitler instructed his generals 'to kill without pity or mercy, all men, women and children of Polish descent or language. Only in this way can we obtain the living space we need.'

Warsaw put up a stout defence (see Campaign 107: *Poland 1939*, Osprey Publishing Ltd: Oxford, 2002, by Steven J. Zaloga), but after a 20-day siege the defenders were forced to surrender. However, it is important to note that the Germans did not fight their way into the city, but instead used their superior artillery and air support to undermine the defence by inflicting heavy civilian casualties. Over 25,000 civilians were killed in this short period and approximately 12 per cent of the city's buildings were destroyed. Unwilling to accept more civilian losses and recognizing that help from the Western Allies was not forthcoming, the Warsaw garrison agreed to capitulate. On 1 October, a company of German infantry marched into the Bruhl Palace, beginning five years of German occupation.

As Poland was succumbing to German aggression, Stalin decided to violate the 1932 Non-Aggression Pact with Poland and ordered the Red Army to invade eastern Poland on 17 September. In short order, Soviet forces overran eastern Poland and captured over 100,000 Polish troops in the process. Britain and France remained silent on Soviet aggression towards their Polish ally. According to the secret provisions of the Molotov–Ribbentrop Pact, Germany occupied western and central Poland, while the Soviet Union occupied eastern Poland.

From the beginning, the Germans used mass murder to terrorize the Polish population. Local *Volksdeutche* formed into *Selbstschutz* (self-defence) units, in conjunction with regular German army units, began a vicious ethnic cleansing operation that murdered over 16,000 Poles by the end of October 1939. In November 1939, the Germans began arresting university professors and closing most schools and churches, in the opening move to crush Poland's identity. Under *Generalplan Ost*, Germany intended first to exploit Poland for forced labour and economic resources to support the Third Reich's war effort. Eventually, the plan envisioned the reduction of the ethnic Polish population down to three to four million within a decade and total extermination within a few decades. German-occupied Poland was divided into two main areas. The Generalgouvernement (General Government, GG) was set up under Governor-General Hans Frank to administer central Poland, including Warsaw. The other main German occupation zone was Reichsgau Wartheland in the western border areas, which was incorporated directly into the Reich in October 1939. In May 1940, Frank began wholesale 'special actions' which resulted in the execution of 7,000 Polish civilians and the imprisonment of thousands more in the Gestapo-run Pawiak Prison in Warsaw.

While the Germans were ransacking western and central Poland, the Soviet occupation was quietly pacifying the eastern occupation zone. Stalin declared Poland non-existent and all people in the occupied area were now Soviet citizens. In the next two years, the Soviets deported over 1.4 million people from eastern Poland to serve as forced labour in the Soviet Union, where two-thirds of them perished. Furthermore, Stalin ordered the elimination of most of the captured Polish military personnel, to inhibit any future anti-Soviet resistance. In March 1940, the Soviet Politburo ordered the execution of 22,000 of the captured Polish military personnel and 40,000 civilians, although their fate was kept secret for years.

THE POLISH RESISTANCE FORMS, 1939–42

Even before Poland was overrun, its General Staff began planning to form an underground resistance movement. While parts of the Polish regular military escaped to continue the fight in France and England, units in Warsaw were ordered to conceal some of their weapons before capitulation. The first resistance movement, the Sluzba Zwyciestwu Polski (Service for Victory in Poland, SZP), consisted of only seven professional army officers, but the SZP reached out to gather in a myriad of amateur resistance groups under its umbrella. In early 1940, the Polish Government-in-exile ordered Pulkownik Stefan Rowecki, former commander of the Warsaw Mechanized Brigade, to form a new resistance group from the SZP, to be known as the Zwiazek Walki Zbrojnej (Union for Armed Struggle, ZWZ). Rowecki proved to be a superb underground leader and it was he who built and founded the organization that eventually became the Armia Krajowa (Home Army, AK) in February 1942. However, there was never a single Polish resistance movement during World War II, mainly owing to the political disunity fostered by opposition to the pre-war Sanacja regime.

Initially, Polish resistance activities were focused on conducting sabotage against German rail traffic passing through Poland, propaganda activities to undermine German morale, clandestine weapons production and intelligence collection. Fortunately, Poland was able to form a strong government-in-exile in London, with Generał dywizji Władysław Sikorski as Prime Minister. In December 1939, Sikorski took direct command of the Polish resistance via radio and declared that the ZWZ 'is a component of the Armed Forces of the Polish Republic'. Couriers made secret runs between London and Warsaw via neutral Turkey, typically requiring three to five weeks, which allowed the government-in-exile to send funds and instructions to the resistance. Initially, the government-in-exile received strong support from the British, in great measure because the Polish regular military provided large numbers of troops to fight under British command. Britain provided training for Polish military personnel, who were then flown by the RAF and inserted by parachute, but relatively few weapons were provided during 1940–43 despite Churchill's orders to the SOE to 'set Europe ablaze'.

ARMIA KRAJOWA VS. THE GERMAN OCCUPATION, 1942–44

While the government-in-exile was trying to form a national resistance, the Germans steadily implemented their *Generalplan Ost* to grind Poland into dust. In 1942, German security forces in Warsaw instituted a tactic known as *Łapanka* ('tag') by Poles; German SS-Polizei and SD Security units would block off a city street and arrest all citizens without a valid *Ausweis* (identity card). Those arrested could be deported to Germany as slave labourers or sent to a local concentration camp. Anywhere from 400 to 1,000 civilians might be arrested in one of these sweeps, which occurred almost daily and discouraged Poles from moving about the streets of their own cities. Altogether, over 1.5 million Poles were kidnapped for forced labour to support the German war effort, which reduced the pool of manpower available to the resistance. In October 1943, SS-Brigadeführer Franz Kutschera authorized street executions in Warsaw, which resulted in the death of about 6,000 civilians. Kutschera also instituted a hostage system to drive a wedge between Polish resistance and people, by executing 100 hostages for each German killed by the AK.

Although the Polish resistance avoided overt confrontations with German occupation forces in 1942–44 in order to conserve its strength for the decisive moment, it was successful in conducting intelligence collection, sabotage and

Wehrmacht troops were fully involved in war crimes in Poland from the outset. Here, troops from the German 29. Infanterie-Division (mot.) survey a mass grave of 300 Polish prisoners from the 74th Infantry Regiment and local civilians, who were executed in early September 1939. (AKG Images, 134344)

SS soldiers escort captured Jewish civilians to the Umschlagplatz rail loading dock for transport to Auschwitz after the destruction of the Warsaw Ghetto in May 1943. (Holocaust Museum, 18192)

assassination missions that undermined the German war effort. The Germans used between 50,000 and 80,000 SS-Polizei and Gestapo to fight a five-year cat and mouse game with the Polish resistance, which succeeded in disrupting the AK from time to time, but failed to destroy it. Rowecki established a reprisal unit, which eventually grew into the Kedyw organization tasked with assassinating senior German occupation leaders responsible for mass murder inside Poland. The most daring AK operation was the assassination of Kutschera in front of his headquarters in Warsaw on 1 February 1944. German figures indicate that between November 1943 and May 1944 the AK killed 704 Germans and wounded 383. Furthermore, the AK also succeeded in sabotaging freight trains passing through Poland, which severely disrupted the German lines of communications to the Eastern Front. Polish intelligence also played a key role in gathering information on the German V-2 rocket programme and passing it to the British.

Despite these successes, the Polish resistance was severely hindered by command and control difficulties, since it couldn't use the telephones or the postal system, both of which were monitored by the Gestapo. Instead, the resistance had to rely on couriers, most of whom were female. The *Łapanka* round-ups were a constant threat to resistance communications and leadership. Nor could the resistance operate effectively in the Warthgau area, owing to the deportation of most of the ethnic Poles – so the AK was constrained to operate primarily in the Generalgouvernement. All the while, the German Gestapo made a major effort to hunt down the AK's leadership and it too, enjoyed some significant successes. On 30 June 1943, Rowecki was betrayed by Gestapo agents and arrested in Warsaw.[1] Pułkownik Bór-Komorowski became the new head of the AK.

Political disunity also hindered the Polish resistance and it was not until February 1942 that the various groups finally began to coalesce into a cohesive national organization. At that time, the AK was the largest group and owed its loyalty to the Polish Government-in-exile. The Bataliony Chłopskie (Peasants' Battalions, BCh) was the second largest group, and it began forming under the aegis of the Stronnictwo Ludowe (People's Party,

---

1 Although under Gestapo interrogation for over a year, Rowecki apparently never revealed any information about the AK's networks.

SL) in 1940 to protect rural areas from German ethnic-cleansing operations. Another large group, the right-wing Narodowe Siły Zbrojne (National Armed Forces, NSZ), was created in 1942 by Pułkownik Ignacy Oziewicz. By 1943, both the BCh and the NSZ were beginning to cooperate with the AK in resistance activities, although they remained in disagreement over political objectives. However, the inclusion of NSZ units into the AK was problematic, since they were overtly anti-Semitic and often pursued their own agenda. Relations between the AK and the communist Armia Ludowa (People's Army, AL) were openly hostile, since the AL sanctioned handing over eastern Poland to the Soviet Union.

One of the early German goals in Warsaw was the eradication of the 400,000 Polish Jews in the city, who comprised nearly one-third of the population. The Germans created the Warsaw Jewish Ghetto in the autumn of 1940 but by 1942 it had served its purpose. In the summer of 1942, the SS began mass deportations from the Warsaw Ghetto to the newly built extermination camps and, in a matter of months, more than three-quarters of the residents were eliminated. However, a small group of residents established the Żydowska Organizacja Bojowa (Jewish Fighting Organization, ZOB) to make a last-ditch stand against the SS. Contact between the AK and the ZOB was difficult owing to the security walls built around the ghetto, but some weapons were smuggled in. While sympathetic to the fighters in the ghetto, Rowecki was unwilling to commit the AK to greater support for what he viewed as a hopeless last stand. The Warsaw Ghetto Uprising began on 19 April 1943 and initially succeeded in evicting the SS troops from the ghetto. However, the result was never in doubt and after 28 days the SS finally crushed the last Jewish resistance. All remaining Jews – except for a thousand or so survivors in hiding or who escaped through sewers – were sent to the death camps and the ghetto was razed.

SOVIET–POLISH POLITICAL RELATIONS, 1939–44

The Soviet Union was in a technical state of war with Poland after 17 September 1939 – a fact conveniently ignored by Britain and the United States. After Operation *Barbarossa* began in 1941, the British Foreign Ministry browbeat the Polish Government-in-exile into re-establishing diplomatic relations with the Soviet Union for the sake of Allied 'unity'. Stalin agreed to re-establish relations in the hope of recruiting Polish troops to fight on the Eastern Front, so he ordered the release of 25,000 Polish soldiers from NKVD prisons and formed a nascent force under Generał dywizji Władysław Anders. However, the Soviet Government feigned ignorance about the location of the remaining 20,000 missing prisoners, indicating to Sikorski's government that Soviet intentions were less than honourable.

The missing Polish officer issue came to a head in April 1943 when the Germans announced the discovery of mass graves near Katyn Forest in the Soviet Union, which were found to contain the corpses of 4,243 Polish officers and NCOs missing since 1939. German propaganda pointed to the Soviets as the culprits of the crime and Poles in both London and Warsaw knew from Anders' men that the victims were last known to be in Soviet custody. Caught red-handed in mass murder, Stalin instead claimed that the SS had executed these prisoners. When Sikorski refused to accept the Soviet version and asked the Red Cross to investigate, the Soviet Union angrily broke off relations with the Polish Government on 26 April and accused it of working with the Nazis. Stalin's hatred for the government-in-exile was unbounded.

On 4 July 1943, Sikorski died in a plane crash at Gibraltar, depriving the government-in-exile of his strong leadership. Although never proven, Sikorski's plane was probably sabotaged and the Soviets had a strong motive to remove him. Sikorski was succeeded by his deputy prime minister, Stanislaw Mikolajczyk, a leader in the pre-war Peasant Party. After being sworn in, Mikolajczyk declared that, 'there is and will be no place in Poland for any kind of totalitarian government in any shape or form'. Despite the fact that Stalin had murdered most of the pre-war Polish Communist Party leadership in 1938, he now decided that he needed a Polish political and military entity under his control as a counterweight to the government-in-exile, whose members were routinely denounced in Soviet propaganda as 'collaborators'. In July 1943, Stalin created the Związek Patriotów Polskich (Union of Polish Patriots, ZPP) in Moscow in order to provide the base for a pro-Soviet puppet regime in Poland after the war. Shortly afterwards, the Soviets also began creating a Polish communist army, known as the Ludowe Wojsko Polskie (Polish People's Army, LWP). The battle lines were drawn.

By September 1943, with the Soviet crossing of the Dnepr River and the Allied landing in Italy, the major Allied powers began making serious plans for post-war Europe. Mikolajczyk knew that the Western Allies were less than eager to protect Poland's rights in political discussions with the Soviets. This was borne out when Polish leaders were excluded from the Tehran Conference in November 1943, even though the issue of Poland's post-war borders was decided. Without consulting or informing any Polish leaders, Churchill and Roosevelt acceded to Stalin's demand that eastern Poland would be given to the Soviet Union. Mikolajczyk sensed that Poland was being sold out by the Western Allies and he repeatedly stated that his government would not accept territorial losses after the war.

On 6 January 1944, the first Red Army units crossed the old pre-war Polish border. Due to the break in diplomatic relations with Moscow, the government-in-exile advised that AK units in these border areas should stay concealed and avoid contact with the Red Army. However, Bór-Komorowski instructed resistance units in these border areas to cooperate with the Soviet troops, if possible. Initially, the Red Army was willing to cooperate with the AK partisan units, since German counterattacks had stalled them on the old Polish border and they needed help. In London, the British urged Mikolajczyk to patch up relations with Stalin prior to the Red Army entering central Poland, but the Soviets made ridiculous demands: discard the pre-war constitution, allow the ZPP to pick a new Polish president, drop any investigation into Katyn Forest and accept the loss of the eastern half of Poland. When Mikolajczyk stubbornly refused to accept the virtual destruction of his government and country, the already tepid British support evaporated.

German officers show the bodies of Polish Generał brigady Mieczysław Smorawinski (commander, II Corps) and Generał dywisji Bronislaw Bohaterewicz to neutral observers at the Katyn Woods inquiry in April 1943. The discovery of this Soviet crime resulted in Stalin angrily breaking off relations with the Polish Government-in-exile. (TRH Cody Images, 1004395)

THE EASTERN FRONT APPROACHES, 1944

When the Soviets began Operation *Bagration* on 23 June 1944 (see Campaign 42: *Bagration 1944,* Osprey Publishing Ltd: Oxford, 1996, by Steven J. Zaloga), quickly shattering the German Heeresgruppe Mitte, the rapidly changing military situation forced the government-in-exile to rethink their relations with the Soviets. In just two weeks, Heeresgruppe Mitte lost about 350,000 troops and 25 of its 33 divisions were shattered. The remnants of Heeresgruppe Mitte fell back into Poland and East Prussia, hotly pursued by the Soviets. By 17 July, Marshal K. Rokossovsky's 1st Belorussian Front had reached Brest-Litovsk, only 187km east of Warsaw. Once firmly established on Polish soil, the Soviets moved rapidly to set up a communist alternative to the government-in-exile, and, on 21 July, the Red Army formed the Polski Komitet Wyzwolenia Narodowego (Polish Committee of National Liberation, PKWN) in the city of Chelm. Soon dubbed the 'Lublin Committee', the PKWN issued a manifesto that claimed that it was 'the only legitimate Polish government'. In London, Mikolajczyk could see the rug being pulled out from under the feet of his government, with his erstwhile allies abandoning Poland to its fate.

As Soviet troops drove deeper into Poland and German resistance continued to crumble, the attitude of the Red Army towards the AK units it encountered changed from cooperation to overt hostility. The NKVD was

The SS Stauferkaserne on Rakowiecka Street in Warsaw. This structure housed the Panzergrenadier replacement battalion for 5. SS-Panzer-Division 'Wiking', as well as a Panzer replacement depot. (Author's collection)

ordered to suppress local AK units once German troops had been defeated in each Soviet-occupied area and 6,000 AK troops were duly arrested in Vilno. Thereafter, it was open season for the NKVD on all Polish resistance forces. On 29 July, large numbers of AK troops were arrested in Lvov and several of their leaders were executed. Both Bór-Komorowski and the government-in-exile were quickly aware of these Soviet actions. The AK also knew that Hitler's own generals had tried to kill him on 20 July and this reinforced the impression that a German collapse was imminent.

Rokossovsky's 1st Belorussian Front achieved a major breakthrough against 4. Panzer-Armee's weak front near Lublin on 22 July and quickly committed the 2nd Tank Army under General-Major Aleksei I. Radzievsky into the 50km-wide gap between 4. Panzer-Armee and 2. Armee Oberkommando (AOK). Radzievsky's tankers advanced over 120km in three days to reach the Vistula River. At the start of the offensive, the 2nd Tank Army consisted of the three tank corps with a total of about 390 T-34-85, 195 M4A2 Sherman and 21 IS-II tanks. While the 8th Guards Army established a bridgehead across the river at Magnuszew, 54km south of Warsaw, the 2nd Tank Army pivoted north-west and headed towards Warsaw. The only German force standing between Warsaw and this advancing tidal wave of Soviet armour was the depleted 73. Infanterie-Division, which had about 2,000 infantry and a few anti-tank guns. On 27 July, 2nd Tank Army routed 73. Infanterie-Division at Garwolin, driving it back towards Warsaw and its division commander was captured. Four days later, the 2nd Tank Army was on the outskirts of Warsaw with over 500 tanks and assault guns still operational. German support units in the area quickly withdrew across the Vistula River and streamed through Warsaw, reinforcing the Polish impression that the Germans were in full retreat. The German mayor of Warsaw had already left the city and German pioneers were observed preparing the Vistula River bridges for demolition. Along Aleje Jerozolimskie[2], Polish girls waved their white handkerchiefs at the columns of retreating German trucks and yelled, '... bye ... bye! Never see you again!' The hour of liberation seemed at hand.

Although Soviet propaganda normally referred to the AK as an 'illegal force', on the night of 29 July, Soviet radio broadcasts urged the AK to rise up and overthrow the German garrison in Warsaw. Soviet leaflets, signed by Foreign Minister Molotov, dropped over the city said, 'Poles! The time of liberation is at hand! Poles, to arms!' The Germans hastily ordered 100,000 Polish civilians in Warsaw to assemble in order to help dig anti-tank ditches around the city, but the AK told civilians to ignore the order. Given this information – that the Germans appeared to be withdrawing, that the Soviets were arresting AK members as they advanced and that the Red Army was virtually at the gates of Warsaw – the government-in-exile and the leadership of the AK judged that the time had come to make their move. Unless some type of Polish political authority was in place in Warsaw before the Soviet arrival, Stalin would claim that the AK had done nothing to liberate Poland and impose the Lublin Committee as the new national government.

The AK leadership in Warsaw had been mulling over the prospects for an uprising for several days, as the news of more German defeats poured in. However, the AK command was divided over the timing of the uprising. A vote taken in an AK council of war on 27 July resulted in a decision to place

2 Jerusalem Avenue, one of the main thoroughfares in Warsaw that goes from Wola to the Vistula River.

Soviet infantry run past a burning Panther tank in Poland during the rapid advance to the Vistula River in late July 1943. (AKG Images, 123589)

the AK on general alert, but revealed five officers in favour of an immediate uprising and five against. Generał brygady Chruściel (Monter) was concerned that his troops lacked sufficient weaponry to begin an uprising until the Germans were clearly pulling out of the city. Pułkownik Iranek-Osmeki, head of intelligence, noted the arrival of German Panzer units in the Warsaw area and also recommended holding off until the Red Army actually occupied Praga. Pułkownik Okulicki, chief of operations disagreed and urged an uprising as soon as Soviet tanks approached the city. Late on the afternoon of 31 July, Monter reported that Soviet tanks had been spotted near Praga. Meanwhile, the government-in-exile left the timing of an uprising up to Bór-Komorowski and its civilian delegate, Jan Jankowski, deferred to military opinion. Finally bowing to pressure to 'do something', Bór-Komorowski made the decision at 1730hrs on 31 July immediately to launch a citywide uprising at 1700hrs on 1 August. Shortly afterwards, Iranek-Osmeki arrived with information that suggested that the Soviet arrival in Praga was not so imminent, but Bór-Komorowski said that it was, 'too late. The order is given. I will not change it.' Unfortunately, the Polish decision-making was based upon the assumptions that the Germans were about to abandon Warsaw, that the Allies would provide vigorous support to an uprising and that the Soviet offensive would continue. All three assumptions were mistaken.

CHRONOLOGY

1939

23 August — Nazi–Soviet Pact signed. Secret protocol divides Poland between them.

1 September — Germans invade western Poland.

17 September — Soviet Union invades eastern Poland, violating 1932 Non-Aggression Pact.

27 September — Warsaw garrison surrenders. German occupation begins.

1940

5 March — Soviet Politburo orders execution of 22,000 captured Polish soldiers.

1941

17 August — Poland and USSR re-establish diplomatic relations.

1942

14 February — Armia Krajowa (AK) is established.

1943

13 April — Germans announce discovery of mass graves of murdered Polish officers in Katyn Forest, pointing to Soviet guilt.

19 April–16 May — Warsaw Ghetto Uprising.

25 April — Soviet Union breaks off relations with Polish Government-in-exile over Katyn Forest allegations.

1944

6 January — Soviet Army first crosses Polish 1939 border.

23 June — The Soviets begin Operation *Bagration* against Heeresgruppe Mitte.

17 July — Soviets arrest about 5,000 AK troops in Vilno

25 July — AK command issues a 'state of alert'. Soviet forces reach the Vistula River south of Warsaw.

29 July — Soviets arrest large number of AK troops in Lvov.

31 July — Soviet tanks spotted near Praga, Bór decides to activate uprising.

1 August — The uprising is planned to begin at 1700hrs but sporadic clashes begin earlier. Fighting breaks out across the city.

4 August — First German reinforcements under SS-Gruppenführer Heinz Reinefarth appear in Wola and Ochota. First Allied airdrop occurs that night.

5 August — Dirlewanger advances into Wola and massacres thousands of civilians.

6 August — Dirlewanger's troops link up with encircled German forces in the Bruhl Palace.

8 August	German forces begin major attacks on the Old Town.
11 August	Polish units abandon Wola and Ochota.
16 August	Germans capture the water filtration plant, interdicting the city's water supply.
19 August	Polish forces abandon the polytechnic after heavy fighting.
20 August	Battalion Kilinski captures the PAST building.
21 August	A major AK attack from Żoliborz and the Old Town against Gdansk railway station is repulsed with heavy losses.
28 August	German forces capture the PWPW Building.
31 August	Last Polish attempt to break through to Old Town from city centre fails.
1–2 September	AK units evacuate the Old Town.
3–6 September	German forces attack and clear out Powisle district.
7–10 September	Germans mount a major attack on the city centre but fail to take much ground.
11 September	Soviet forces resume offensive against German forces east of Vistula. Germans begin attack on Czerniaków district.
13 September	Germans blow up the Vistula bridges.
14 September	Praga falls to Soviet forces.
15 September	A Polish (LWP) battalion crosses into Czerniaków and links up with AK units.
16 September	Soviet airdrops into Warsaw begin.
18 September	US bombers fly major air resupply mission to Warsaw.
23 September	Resistance ends in Czerniaków.
24–26 September	Germans capture most of Mokotów in an all-out assault.
28–29 September	A major German attack on Żoliborz captures most of the district.
30 September	AK envoys arrive at German headquarters to begin surrender talks.
2 October	Polish emissaries sign the capitulation document.
4 October	AK forces march out of Warsaw into captivity.

1945

17 January	Soviet forces occupy the ruins of Warsaw.

OPPOSING LEADERS

POLISH

Generał brygady Count Tadeusz Bór-Komorowski, commander of the AK. (Jozef Pilsudski Institute)

Generał brygady Count Tadeusz Komorowski (1895–1966), better known by the name Bór-Komorowski, was commander of the AK. During World War I, Komorowski served as an officer in the Austro-Hungarian Army and then joined the post-war Polish Army. In the inter-war period, he was a career cavalry officer who led the Polish equestrian team in the 1936 Berlin Olympics and then commanded the Grudziadz Cavalry School. During the 1939 Polish campaign, Pułkownik Komorowski took command of the remnants of several cavalry formations and briefly fought Soviet units entering Eastern Poland. After Poland's occupation, Komorowski avoided arrest and functioned as one of the organizers of the Polish underground in the Kraków area for 18 months, despite a massive Gestapo effort to hunt him down. In July 1941 he became deputy commander of the AK and succeeded Generał brygady Rowecki in July 1943. Although Komorowski was very effective as a conspirator, his abilities as a tactical commander were limited by old-fashioned thinking; for example, he had never used a radio to command troops prior to the Warsaw Uprising and he was ineffectual in coordinating the AK forces outside the city to assist those forces operating inside the city. After the uprising, Bór-Komorowski went into internment in Germany at Oflag IV-C. He was liberated at the end of the war and spent the rest of his life in London, where he served as Prime Minister of the Polish Government-in-exile, in 1947–49.

Generał brygady Antoni Chruściel (Monter) (1895–1960) was de facto commander of all the armed forces in the Warsaw Uprising of 1944, as well as the AK's chief of staff. He served in the Austro-Hungarian Army on the Eastern Front in 1914–18, rising from private to company commander. Like Bór, he then joined the new Polish Army and fought in the Russo-Polish War. By 1938, he took command of the 82nd Infantry Regiment and his unit was near the border on 1 September 1939. Pułkownik Chruściel's regiment fought a delaying action, falling back towards Warsaw but was trapped west of the capital at Modlin and forced to surrender. Chruściel was released a few weeks later and he went to Warsaw and joined the Zwiazek Walki Zbrojnej (ZWZ) underground organization in June 1940. A year later, he was appointed commander of the AK's Warsaw district. During the uprising, Chruściel proved to be a tough and stubborn infantry leader who refused to give in to the inevitable. After the Warsaw Uprising, Chruściel was interned in Stalag

XIII-D and then the famous Oflag IV-C at Colditz Castle. Liberated by the Americans in May 1945, Chruściel joined the Polish II Corps and served in the Polish Army in the West until it was demobilized by the British in 1948. Although initially Chruściel planned to return to Soviet-held Poland, he was deprived of Polish citizenship by the communist authorities of Poland and had to remain in exile. Upon demobilization he first settled in London but later moved to Washington, DC, where he died in 1960.

Pułkownik Jan Mazurkiewicz (Radoslaw) (1896–1988) was commander of the 2,300-man Group Radoslaw, one of the best-trained and equipped units in the AK. Like many AK leaders, Mazurkiewicz had fought in the Polish Legion in World War I and then in the Russo-Polish War in 1920. He joined the resistance in 1940 and the Kedyw in 1943. After the war, the communists imprisoned him.

GERMAN

General der Panzertruppen Nikolaus von Vormann (1895–1959) was commander of 9. AOK from 27 June 1944. Vormann joined the German Army as a volunteer in August 1914 and was commissioned an infantry *Leutnant* in 1915. During World War II, Vormann served primarily in staff assignments in 1939–42, but in December 1942 he was given command of 23. Panzer-Division and later XLVII Panzer-Korps during the relief effort for the Korsun Pocket in February 1944. Nominally in command of Wehrmacht forces in the Warsaw area, Vormann was pushed aside by the SS during the suppression of the uprising and he was unhappy with the rogue SS units operating within his area of command responsibility. Just before the end of the uprising, Vormann was relieved of command and replaced by General der Panzertruppen Smilo Freiherr von Lüttwitz.

SS-Obergruppenführer Erich von dem Bach (1899–1972) was born in Pomerania of mixed Polish–German stock. He joined the Prussian Army as a volunteer in December 1914, was commissioned a *Leutnant* in 1916, wounded twice, gassed in 1918 and awarded the Iron Cross twice. Bach was forced to resign from the Reichsheer in 1924 because of political intrigues and he switched to the Border Guards. He joined the SS in 1931, was promoted to SS-Brigadeführer in 1933 and then participated in the infamous 'Night of the Long Knives' in 1934. By 1937 he was the SS and police leader in Silesia. It was Bach's initiative to establish Auschwitz concentration camp in Poland in May 1940.

SS-Obergruppenführer Erich von dem Bach, in overall command of German forces tasked with crushing the Warsaw Uprising. (Bundesarchiv, 183-S73507)

In June 1941, Bach was put in charge of SS-Polizei units operating behind Heeresgruppe Mitte in the Soviet Union and eventually took control over a slurry of anti-partisan units. SS troops under Bach's command were responsible for the mass murder of 35,000 civilians in Riga and by 1943 had murdered 200,000 more in Belarus and Eastern Poland. After the destruction of Heeresgruppe Mitte in July 1944, Bach's command retreated into Poland and on 2 August 1944, he took command of all troops fighting against the Warsaw Uprising (Korpsgruppe Bach). After the uprising was crushed, Bach was awarded the Knight's Cross and later commanded a corps on the Oder River line in 1945. During the post-war Nuremberg Trials, Bach turned witness for the prosecution against Himmler and Göring to save his own neck and got off with only four years in prison. However, in 1958 German courts convicted him of crimes committed against German citizens during the 1930s and he died in prison.

SS-Gruppenführer Heinrich Reinefarth (1903–79) joined the Nazi Party and the SS in 1932. Reinefarth was drafted as a reserve NCO at the start of World War II and was awarded the Iron Cross 2nd Class for service in Poland. He served with the Waffen-SS during the campaign in the West in 1940 and was awarded the Knight's Cross. After France, Reinefarth was promoted very quickly and on 20 April 1942, he was promoted to SS-Brigadeführer. In January 1944 Reinefarth was assigned as commander of SS and Police in Reichsgau Wartheland and was responsible for forced deportation of thousands of Poles. Once the Warsaw Uprising began, Reinefarth organized an *Einsatzgruppe* composed of SS-Polizei and SD security units and led it to the city to mount the first counterattacks. Reinefarth's troops were responsible for the execution of about 50,000 civilians in the city, including the 'Wola Massacre'. Owing to his ruthless suppression of the uprising, Reinefarth was awarded the Oak Leaves to his Iron Cross. After the Warsaw Uprising, Reinefarth commanded Festung Küstrin in early 1945 but disobeyed orders to fight to the death and escaped westwards. After the war, the Polish communist regime demanded his extradition but the Western Allies declined in order to use him as a witness in the Nuremberg Trials. Reinefarth never paid for his crimes and he even served in the state legislature of Schleswig-Holstein in 1962–67.

SS-Oberführer d.R. Oskar Dirlewanger, commander of SS-Sonderregiment Dirlewanger, a special anti-partisan unit that was responsible for many of the worst atrocities committed in Warsaw. (Bundesarchiv, 183-S73495)

SS-Oberführer d.R. Oskar Dirlewanger (1895–1945), commander of SS-Sonderregiment Dirlewanger. Dirlewanger entered the army in 1913 and was commissioned as an infantry officer in 1915. He had a distinguished war record, fighting on both the Western and Eastern fronts in World War I, being wounded six times and receiving the Iron Cross First Class. After the war he joined the Freikorps and fought communists, found time to obtain a PhD in

SS-Brigadeführer Bronislav Vladislavovich Kaminski, commander of the Russian volunteer RONA brigade that was absorbed into the SS in 1944. Owing to his inability to keep his undisciplined troops in hand during operations in Warsaw, he was executed on Reichsführer Himmler's orders. (Bundesarchiv, 101I-280-1075-17A)

Major Max Reck, commander of Kampfgruppe Reck. (Author's collection)

political science from the University of Frankfurt in 1922 and then joined the Nazi Party. After participating in Hitler's 1923 Beer Hall Putsch, Dirlewanger drifted for a few years before joining the SA in 1932 and the party rewarded him with a sinecure in the Labour Department. However, Dirlewanger was a self-destructive drunk who argued with his superiors and then went on a drinking binge after the Rohm putsch in July 1934 in which he sexually molested a 14-year-old female cadet in a party-owned automobile, then crashed the car and injured the girl. It was a Chappaquiddick-style gaffe that even the Nazi Party, tolerant to the antics of war veterans, could not ignore. Dirlewanger was sentenced to two years in prison and expelled from the Nazi Party. After being released in 1936, some of Dirlewanger's old SA cronies encouraged him to volunteer for the German Condor Legion in Spain, where he served for 16 months and was wounded three times. Dirlewanger returned to Germany at the start of the war but was not allowed to join the Waffen-SS until June 1940. Thereafter, Dirlewanger was entrusted with forming a small anti-partisan unit composed of petty criminals and this battalion-sized unit initially operated in southern Poland during 1941. In Poland and White Russia, Dirlewanger demonstrated a taste for corrupt and sadistic behaviour, including numerous atrocities against civilians. Dirlewanger was in Berlin at the start of the Warsaw Uprising and, although ordered to proceed directly to the city by Himmler, he dawdled and earned himself another reprimand. Dirlewanger was an undisciplined, degenerate butcher, but he was also a fearless sociopath who loved to fight, which made him useful to the Waffen-SS. Dirlewanger gained the Knight's Cross for his role in suppressing the uprising. However, Dirlewanger did not escape justice and after the war he was indicted for war crimes and then beaten to death in prison.

SS-Brigadeführer Bronislav Vladislavovich Kaminski (1899–1944) was the commander of the Russkaya Osvoboditelnaya Narodnaya Armiya (RONA) unit. He was born in St Petersburg of mixed German–Polish parentage and served in the Red Army during the Russian Civil War, but was arrested and imprisoned during the purge of 1937. Freed by the German invasion, Kaminski eventually took charge of an anti-communist Russian militia force around Bryansk, dubbed RONA. He also established the semi-autonomous Lokot Republic in Bryansk, which cooperated with the Germans. As the Soviets advanced westwards, Kaminski's unit was forced to relocate and was absorbed into the SS. Owing to his unruly behaviour in the Warsaw Uprising, he was executed on the orders of Himmler on 28 August 1944.

Generalmajor Günter Rohr (1893–??), commander of Kampfgruppe Rohr in the Warsaw Uprising. Rohr was commissioned an infantry *Leutnant* just before World War I but saw little active service. He was plagued by ill health during the 1920s, which held back his career. Rohr missed the Polish campaign in 1939 but distinguished himself as commander of 16. Infanterie-Division at the battle of Stonne in May 1940. Thereafter, Rohr spent over a year as commandant of Saarbrucken in 1940–41, returning briefly to infantry commands with Heeresgruppe Mitte in 1941–43. However, Rohr spent much of 1942–43 on sick leave in the Führer Reserve and thereafter commanded a coastal defence unit near Genoa, Italy. In June 1944, Rohr was brought back to the Eastern Front to command Festung Lemberg. Plagued by rheumatism and lacking any experience in urban combat or counter-insurgency, Rohr was a poor choice as a *Kampfgruppe* commander in Warsaw.

Major Max Reck (1911–??), commander of Kampfgruppe Reck from 5 August 1944. After joining the army in 1929, Reck rose to the rank of *Oberfeldwebel* by the start of the war. Reck was promoted to *Leutnant* in Infanterie-Regiment 236 of 69. Infanterie-Division in March 1940 and participated in the landing at Oslo in April 1940. After being wounded twice in the Norwegian campaign, Reck spent most of 1940–42 in garrison duty in Norway. He was given an infantry battalion command with the 6. Infanterie-Division in Heeresgruppe Mitte in October 1942, but was wounded during the Soviet Orel counteroffensive in July 1943. In late 1943, the recuperating Major Reck was sent to train infantry cadets at the infantry school at Posen, which is where he was just prior to the Warsaw Uprising.

Oberst Willy Schmidt, commander of Sicherungs-Regiment 608. (Author's collection)

Oberst Willy Schmidt (1892–??), commander of the Sicherungs-Regiment 608 from July 1942. Schmidt joined the German Army as a volunteer in 1911 and was promoted to *Leutnant* in the infantry in 1915. After World War I, Schmidt left the army and became a businessman but was recalled to active duty in 1935. At the start of the war he was an infantry battalion commander in 86. Infanterie-Division on the Saar Front and his unit followed the Panzers through the Ardennes during the 1940 French campaign. After a year of occupation duty in Belgium in 1940–41, Schmidt was given command of Infanterie-Regiment 426 in 126. Infanterie-Division of Heeresgruppe Nord in November 1941 and was involved in the fierce fighting on the Volkhov Front. However, Schmidt fell ill after four months in command and was sent back to Germany to recuperate. Apparently judged no longer healthy enough for front-line infantry command, Schmidt was assigned to command a security regiment fighting Soviet partisans.

Generalleutnant Rainer Stahel (1892–1955), city commandant of Warsaw, 25 July to 25 August 1944. Stahel served in the infantry in World War I and was afterwards released to serve in the Finnish Army in the post-war period. He joined the Luftwaffe in 1935 and served in command of various flak units in France, Italy and the Eastern Front up to 1943. In October 1943, was made city commandant of Rome for eight months and then brought back to the Eastern Front to organize the defence of Vilna against Soviet spearheads. Stahel was awarded the Swords to his Knight's Cross for his actions at Vilna and he was then sent to Warsaw to stabilize the situation there, but arrived only the day before the uprising began. During the uprising, Stahel was cut off in his headquarters in the Saxon Palace, which made it possible for Bach to take control over all German military and police units operating in the city. Stahel was then sent to Romania where he had the misfortune to arrive just as it was switching sides and he was handed over to the NKVD. Stahel spent the rest of his life as a prisoner in the Gulag.

OPPOSING FORCES

POLISH

Armia Krajowa (Home Army, AK)

This was the typical uniform for Kedyw troops in the Warsaw Uprising – German steel helmet, camouflaged SS smock, pre-war Polish belt and trousers and leather boots. The weapon is a 9mm Steyr MP34 sub-machine gun, which was used by SS-Polizei units. (Author's collection)

The AK was built by professional army officers, most of whom had served in the Polish Legions in World War I, but it was primarily composed of enthusiastic amateurs with little formal military training or experience. Since it was formed as a clandestine network that was constantly being hunted by the Gestapo, the AK was not built like a normal military organization but rather in a cellular manner so that the arrest of individual leaders would not compromise large units. Thus before the uprising, most members knew only a handful of their fellow soldiers. The basic unit was the platoon and larger units – companies, battalions and brigades – did not assemble in Warsaw until the uprising began.

By July 1944, the AK reached its peak strength and Bór claimed that it had 380,000 members nationwide and 48,000 in the Warsaw area (including 4,300 in the Wojskowa Sluzba Kobiet, Women's Auxiliary Service, WSK). Each of the eight AK districts in the Warsaw area had from three to 12 battalion-sized units, which operated under the control of a district commander. Each AK battalion typically had three or four companies and a total strength of 200–600 fighters. In addition to the AK, there were also about 4,000 insurgents provided by the right-wing NSZ, the Communist AL, the Socialist militia (PPS) and several other smaller groups that more or less cooperated with the AK during the uprising.

Training and discipline were uneven across the AK, as befits a citizen-based militia, but the most effective units were the Kedyw and Scout battalions. The Kedyw (Kierownictwo Dywersji, Directorate of Sabotage and Diversion) units were formed in rural areas outside Warsaw in early 1943, primarily to conduct sabotage and assassination missions. Personnel for the Kedyw units were recruited from the Zwiazek Harcestwa Ploskiego (Polish Scouts, ZHP), which had been outlawed by the German occupation, and its leaders were often Cichociemni (silent dark ones) Special Forces troops flown in from Britain. Once suppressed, the ZHP evolved into the covert Szare Szeregi (Grey Ranks) scouting organization, which included male and female members from 12 to 18 years of age, and which conducted vital intelligence collection and sabotage for the AK. Older scouts joined the Grupy Szturmowe (Assault Groups, GS), which were subordinate to the Kedyw. Just before the uprising, most of the Kedyw and Szare Szeregi units were brought into

A Polish-made 9mm Sten Mark II sub-machine gun (left) and 9mm Błyskawica sub-machine gun (right). At the start of the uprising, the AK had at least 650 SMGs in Warsaw. (Author's collection)

Warsaw and formed into battalions Zoska, Parasol, Wigry and Miotla. The other elite unit in the AK was Regiment Baszta, which began forming as a security force in 1939 to guard resistance leaders, and eventually grew to a three-battalion regiment with 2,200 fighters

The AK never had enough weapons or ammunition to fight a conventional battle. Weapons came from three primary sources: from within Poland, from Britain and equipment acquired from the Germans. A significant amount of weapons from the Polish Regular Army had been buried in 1939, but five years later many of these hidden stockpiles had either deteriorated or were difficult to recover. Nevertheless, the AK was able to retrieve small quantities of wz.28 automatic rifles, 7.92mm wz.35 anti-tank rifles, 7.92mm ckm wz.30 machine guns (Browning M1917), a few light mortars and hundreds of 7.92mm wz.29 carbines (Mauser 98K). The Polish resistance was able to establish several underground weapons factories, which produced a wide range of light weapons, often by using parts from civilian industries. By August 1944, the AK produced about one-third of its own weapons, including flame-throwers, Filipinka and Sidolówka hand grenades, about 600 9mm Blyskawica (Lightning) sub-machine guns and several hundred 9mm ViS wz.35 pistols. Surprisingly, the AK was able to purchase a significant number of weapons from corrupt German officials; in 1943 alone, using currency supplied from London, the AK was able to buy nine heavy and 13 light machine guns, 18 machine pistols, 424 rifles and 881 pistols. When Bór-Komorowski decided to initiate active partisan operations in eastern Poland in early 1944, he directed that many weapons be sent to arm the AK units there, which severely depleted the stockpile remaining in Warsaw. Furthermore, owing to poor staff work the AK did not always make the best use of its available resources – in 1947 a cache of 678 Sten guns was found in Warsaw and apparently the weapons had never been issued to the AK during the uprising.

Although the first 'air bridge' was established to Poland in 1941, the British Special Operations Executive (SOE) never made serious efforts to ship large amounts of weapons to Poland. Royal Air Force aircraft losses on these early missions were significant and the SOE was focused on supporting insurgencies in Western Europe. In January 1944, the RAF moved the Polish

A Stuka dive-bombing a target near Krakowskie Przedmiescie. German airpower was so limited over Warsaw that its main contribution was in terms of inflicting collateral damage that sapped Polish morale, rather than providing direct tactical support. (Warsaw Uprising Museum, MPW-IN/2992)

Special Duties Flight 1586 with its six bombers to Brindisi in southern Italy, ostensibly to better support the AK but in fact the planes were often diverted to other missions. Up until July 1944, RAF planes delivered about 600 tons of weapons to Poland by parachute, including 8,900 9mm Sten Mk II sub-machine guns, 9,200 other firearms, 314 PIAT anti-tank launchers, seven light mortars and 30.8 tons of plastic explosives. However, virtually all of the British-supplied weapons went to rural drop zones outside Warsaw and could not easily be brought into the city, where large stockpiles were more vulnerable to detection. In the spring of 1944, the Gestapo located two of the AK's largest arsenals, capturing about 20 per cent of the AK's weapons. In response, Bór-Komorowski ordered much of the weaponry dispersed to rural areas, which increased security but which made it difficult to retrieve in time for the uprising. Although it is now clear that the AK leadership was unsure about exactly how many weapons it had in Warsaw at the start of the uprising, it had at least 39 heavy machine guns, 130 light machine guns, 2,629 rifles, 657 sub-machine guns, 3,846 pistols, 30 flame-throwers, six mortars, 21 PIAT anti-tank launchers, 44,000 grenades and 12,000 Molotov cocktails. Monter and his staff had not ensured a fair distribution of the available weapons, so elite units such as Regiment Baszta and Kedyw had weapons for about 25–30 per cent of their troops, while other units had only token armament. One of the best-equipped units, the 1st Company of Battalion Zaremba, had one ckm machine gun, three rkm automatic rifles, 50 carbines and 80 pistols for its 350 soldiers – a 38 per cent armed rate. Bór-Komorowski estimated that his troops had 100 rounds per machine gun and

30 per pistol. It is unlikely that the AK ever had more than 10,000 armed troops active in Warsaw at one time throughout the battle, but they were able to carefully conserve their limited ammunition stocks and they never ran out of ammunition in 63 days of fighting.

While the AK fought as insurgents, they made great efforts to be recognized as legitimate combatants. Most AK fighters wore either civilian clothes or pieces of captured German uniforms, with only WP (Polish Army) armbands or Polish eagles on their caps to denote their affiliation. Uniforms included a mix of pre-war Polish uniform items, captured German helmets and Waffen-SS camouflage smocks (dubbed *Panterki*). During the uprising, large stocks of Luftwaffe coveralls and field caps were captured and they were dyed black, which became standard wear for AK troops in the southern parts of the city. One unit even wore blue postal office uniforms. Although the Germans regarded the AK troops as bandits, their use of visible rank and national insignia as well as a recognizable command structure afforded them rights under the Geneva Convention, recognition of which the government-in-exile was quick to demand of both Germany and the Soviet Union. Women and children also played major roles in the AK, particularly as scouts and couriers.

Overall, the AK units at district level were best suited for static defensive operations and the only units with any offensive capability were the Kedyw and Szare Szeregi battalions, which remained under central command. Once most of central Warsaw was liberated, the AK should have been able to use its interior lines to shift its reserves to meet attacks on the peripheries, but this proved very difficult in practice. Throughout the uprising, the AK was handicapped by very poor tactical command and control, which made it almost impossible for its leadership to mass its forces or coordinate actions in different parts of the city. Some units did have captured German field telephones and a few field radios were provided from England, but Monter primarily relied on couriers to relay orders. Instead, each sector essentially fought a piecemeal battle and died alone. On the other hand, the AK's strategic communications were quite good. Throughout most of the uprising, Bór-Komorowski was able to remain in radio contact with London, which was better than the British 1st Airborne Division was able to do at Arnhem in September 1944.

Ludowe Wojsko Polskie (Polish People's Army, LWP)

Generał Berling's 1st Polish Army of the LWP played a minor role in the closing weeks of the uprising. Although formed from Polish prisoners in the Soviet Union, more than half of the officers in the LWP were either Red Army or NKVD in order to ensure its submission to Soviet objectives. Once the Red Army entered Poland, the NKVD arrested a significant number of AK members and many were forced to join the 1st Polish Army. The 1st Polish Army did not arrive in Praga until 14 September. Although elements of three LWP divisions tried to cross the Vistula River on 15–19 September, the equivalent of only four rifle battalions actually made it across. These battalions crossed with light weapons and received no significant artillery support from the 1st Polish Army. After the units were decimated in a few days of fighting, the remaining personnel and equipment were absorbed into local AK units. The only tangible battlefield effect of the LWP reinforcements was to prolong Polish resistance in the Czerniaków District along the river for a few extra days.

Ten Sturmpanzer IVs (often called Brummbären after the war) moved to Warsaw as Sturmpanzer Kompanie z.b.V. 218 on 13 August 1944. These assault guns were armed with a 150mm howitzer that could demolish most buildings. (HITM Archives)

GERMAN

The suppression of the Warsaw Uprising was the only major German ground combat operation in World War II that was run almost entirely by the SS. Although the operation occurred in the 9. AOK area, Hitler and Himmler directed the SS to suppress the revolt and initially it was viewed as a 'special action' on a citywide scale. It was only when it became obvious that the hotchpotch of SS and Police units assembled were inadequate for real city fighting that more conventional units were drawn into the battle.

From the beginning, the Germans were handicapped by their lack of high-quality infantry and were forced to rely on firepower. Most of the infantry that was available – SS-Polizei, raw recruits from Wehrkreis XXI training units and Landesschützen militia – used inept street-fighting tactics and suffered crippling losses as a result. Lack of experienced junior-level leadership in the ad hoc units thrown together to suppress the uprising greatly reduced the combat effectiveness of these formations. The total German garrison in Warsaw at the start of the uprising amounted to about 16,000 personnel, but most were dispersed in small garrisons and only about 5,000 were available to defend the Police District. While the German-held facilities were fairly well protected by obstacles and machine-gun bunkers, most of the troops inside them were capable only of static defence and relied on reinforcements from outside the city to crush the resistance.

SS and foreign units

SS-Sonderregiment Dirlewanger was initially formed as a company-sized unit from former poachers in July 1940, with the idea that they would be adept at hunting partisans in the forests of Poland. After misbehaving badly in Poland, the unit was shipped to White Russia to fight Soviet partisans in March 1942 and was soon upgraded to battalion size. From March 1942 to

June 1944, Sonderbataillon Dirlewanger was involved in 19 anti-partisan operations in the Minsk area, killing thousands of partisans and civilians. The battalion just managed to avoid annihilation at Minsk once the Soviets began Operation *Bagration*, and it was pulled back to East Prussia to reorganize as a regiment. The regiment arrived by truck in Warsaw on 4 August and consisted of 881 men in two battalions, a heavy machine-gun company, a mortar company and an anti-tank platoon. SS-Sonderregiment Dirlewanger was primarily equipped with captured Russian weapons and it had never been regarded as capable of front-line service. By the time of the Warsaw Uprising, the personnel composition of the regiment was 45 per cent German ex-convicts, 40 per cent former concentration camp inmates, 10 per cent Ukrainian volunteers and five per cent SS regulars.

The Waffen-Sturm-Brigade RONA (Russkaya Osvoboditelnaya Narodnaya Armiya), aka the Kaminski Brigade, evolved from a local anti-communist militia in the Bryansk area in 1941–42 to a fully fledged unit in the Waffen-SS by July 1944. Although the brigade had 4,000–5,000 members, only a 1,700-man *Kampfgruppe* with four T-34 tanks, one SU-76 assault gun and two 122mm howitzers was sent to Warsaw. The Kaminski Brigade was a relatively cohesive unit on its home soil, but once it was forced to evacuate westwards as a result of Operation *Bagration*, its morale quickly plummeted. Furthermore, the unit had received only rudimentary training and lacked sufficient junior leaders who could keep the men in hand. In Warsaw, the troops regarded themselves as unleashed to pillage and rape, rather than to conduct intensive house-to-house fighting and even Bach quickly recognized that this unit was more of a liability than an asset.

The SS provided one Azerbaijani battalion, one mixed Caucasian battalion and the well-regarded Armenian–Georgian II./Gebirgsjäger-Regiment 'Bergmann' to supplement Dirlewanger's regiment. While the Azerbaijani battalion and Eastern Muslim battalions were low-quality units formed from former Soviet POWs in 1942–43, the Armenian unit had been

A German SdKfz 251/1-II half-track equipped with Wurfrahmen 40 28/32cm rockets. The Poles dubbed these weapons 'mooing cows' owing to the sound their rockets made and they were a deadly threat to exposed personnel. (Bundesarchiv, 696/435/11a)

formed from volunteers and organized by the Abwehr's Brandenbergers to conduct anti-partisan operations. Several SS replacement units were also used in Warsaw, including a company of officer cadets. Perhaps the oddest unit in this hotchpotch collection of unique formations was the schwere SS-Kompanie Rontgen-Posen, formed from X-Ray technicians and medical personnel from an SS hospital in Posen. The SS also had seven Russian and Cossack battalion-sized units available – a total of about 5,000 troops – but these units were so unruly and undisciplined that they spent most of the battle in reserve and were used only sparingly.

Wehrmacht units

Initially, the German 9. AOK had few combat troops involved in suppressing the Warsaw Uprising, but it was required to provide a number of combat support units suited for city fighting. Indeed, the SS *Kampfgruppen* in Warsaw would not have been able to make much progress without the support of army assault guns, artillery and pioneers. However, as SS losses mounted, Wehrkreis XXI (Posen) was ordered to dip into its Replacement Army formations and it sent three infantry training battalions to Warsaw.

Two companies of Armee-Panzerjäger-Bataillon 743 equipped with 28 of the new Hetzer tank destroyers were stationed in Warsaw at the start of the uprising and they were quickly pressed into the infantry support role. This unit belonged to 9. AOK but was taken over by Kampfgruppe Reinefarth for much of August. However, the Hetzer proved to have difficulty fighting in tight quarters since the entire vehicle had to be turned to engage targets and its 75mm gun was not powerful enough to destroy reinforced buildings; in September 1944 the battalion was reassigned for its intended role with IV SS-Panzer Korps. Another unit acquired from 9. AOK, Panzerabteilung 302 (Fkl), was a radio-controlled tank battalion that had 24 StuG III assault guns used as control vehicles and about 50 Goliath and B IV remote control demolition vehicles. The Goliath would prove particularly useful in destroying Polish barricades, but there were not enough to go around.

Several new weapons, specifically designed for city fighting after experience gained from the battle of Stalingrad, were sent to Warsaw. The Sturmtiger, an assault gun built on a Tiger tank chassis, was armed with a 380mm rocket launcher that could fire high-explosive or shaped-charge rockets capable of demolishing a typical building or penetrating reinforced concrete structures. Two Sturmtigers were formed into Panzer Sturm-Mörser Kompanie 1000 and fought in Warsaw from 19–28 August 1944. Warsaw also saw the first real combat use of the Sturmpanzer IV,[3] an assault gun armed with a 150mm howitzer on a PzKpfw IV chassis. Ten Sturmpanzer IVs were formed into Sturmpanzer-Kompanie z.b.V. 218 and moved to Warsaw on 13 August.

Initially, the only engineer unit in Warsaw was the Pioniere-Bataillon 654, which was assigned to guard the bridges over the Vistula. Although these pioneers were pressed into street-fighting duties early in the uprising, they lacked the specialized equipment for this mission. By 11 August, the Germans had brought in Pionier-Sturm-Bataillon 500, which had two companies equipped with 18 Sdkfz-1 half-tracks (including eight Flammpanzerwagen equipped with flame-throwers). This unit also had one Taifun platoon equipped with a powerful new type of fuel-air explosive.

---

3 Often called the Brummbär (grizzly bear) in post-war descriptions but this term was not in use in 1944.

The Germans had relatively little artillery available to suppress the Warsaw Uprising. They did have armoured engineer companies from Fallschirm-Panzer-Division 1 'Hermann Göring' and 19. Panzer-Division, which had SdKfz 251/1-II half-tracks equipped with Wurfrahmen 40 28/32cm rockets. The Poles dubbed these mobile rocket launchers 'mooing cows' and they were capable of laying down barrages of high-explosive or incendiary rockets against an area target. Schwere Stellungs-Werfer-Batterie 201, a fixed rocket-launcher unit, set up a firing position in the Saxon Gardens, where it could hurl up to 40 incendiary or high-explosive rockets in a salvo out to 1,500m. During much of the uprising, the Germans parked Eisbahn Panzerzug 75, mounting four 105mm howitzers, on the Citadel Bridge and used it to shell AK forces in the Old Town. Otherwise, Vormann provided the SS with only one battery each of 105mm and 150mm howitzers, two 210mm mortars and two 280mm howitzers.

In order to assist in the destruction of Warsaw, Hitler ordered the dispatch of three 600mm 'Karl' super-heavy mortars to reinforce Korpsgruppe von dem Bach. The first mortar, 'Ziu', was sent to Warsaw from 17 August to 22 September 1944, forming Heeres Artillerie Batterie 638. Two more heavy mortars, 'Rex' and 'Thor', were formed into Heeres Artillerie Batterie 428 sent to Warsaw on 7–10 September and remained until October. The 'Karl' batteries operated from Wolski Park, on the western edge of the city. At least 56 600mm mortar rounds were fired into Warsaw during the uprising. Although 'Karl' was not accurate enough to engage point targets, its 1.7-ton shells could reduce any building it hit to rubble and served to terrorize the defenders. However, 'Karl' experienced a high 'dud' rate during the uprising – its shells were designed to penetrate reinforced concrete not thin-skinned apartment buildings – and the Poles were able to retrieve explosives from the shells and use them as filler for hand grenades.

Luftwaffe units

The Luftwaffe's Fallschirm-Panzer-Division 1 'Hermann Göring' played a major role in both stopping the initial Soviet drive on Warsaw and in the final stages of the suppression of the uprising. Generalmajor Wilhelm Schmalz's division had just arrived in the Warsaw area from Italy and was still incomplete. On 1 August 1944, the bulk of the division was located north-east of Praga but one Panzer battalion, with 20 PzKpfw IV tanks, was still unloading in Warsaw when the uprising began.

By the time of the Warsaw Uprising, the Luftwaffe had long since lost control over the skies on the Eastern Front. Generaloberst Ritter von Greim's Luftflotte VI based in Poland was reduced to only 252 aircraft by the end of July 1944. Furthermore, fuel shortages crippled operations, permitting only a few of the available aircraft to fly sorties. Just six days before the Warsaw Uprising began, American P-38 and P-51 fighters conducting shuttle raids to Ukrainian bases intercepted SG 77 over eastern Poland and shot down 27 of its 44 Stukas in a virtual massacre. Nevertheless, the Soviet decision to suspend its air activity over the Warsaw area during the uprising and their refusal to allow Allied use of their bases in the Ukraine enabled the Luftwaffe to provide a limited amount of air support. The main unit used was Leutnant Hans-Jürgen Klussmann's four Ju-87 Stukas from 1./SG 1 based at Okecie airfield, which flew 711 of 1,204 total Stuka sorties during the battle. Although Stuka attacks in Warsaw were terrifying for the civilian population, they had only limited effect on dug-in AK units.

ORDERS OF BATTLE, 1 AUGUST 1944

POLISH

Number in parentheses indicates number of companies in this formation

NOTE: The Polish OB fluctuated considerably during the course of the uprising. Some units, such as Group Chrobry II that began as a two-battalion formation were later consolidated into a single battalion as losses occurred. Other units that began as company-sized formations were later upgraded to battalions. Unit names also changed as various leaders became casualties. Thus, some units mentioned in the narrative in the September fighting will not correspond exactly with the 1 August 1944 order of battle.

OLD TOWN (STARE MIASTO)

Group Rog
- Battalion Boncza (four)
- Battalion Gustaw-Harnas (four)
- Battalion Wigry (three)
- Battalion Dzik
- Group PWB/17/5
- One platoon of AL

Group Kuba-Sosna
- Battalion Gozdawa (three)
- Battalion Lukasinski (six)
- Battalion Chrobry I (four)
- KB Battalion Nalecz

Group Lesnik (three)

CITY CENTRE

Western Section
- Battalion Zaremba-Piorun (three)
- Battalion Golski (five)

Northern Section
- Battalion Belt (three)
- Battalion Milosz (three)
- Battalion Iwo (four)
- Battalion Ruczaj (four)
- KB Battalion Sokol (two)

Eastern Section/Czerniaków
- Group Kryska
  - Battalion Tur
  - Battalion Tum
  - Battalion Stefan

UNDER CENTRAL COMMAND:

Group Radoslaw
- Battalion Miotla/Czata 49 (three)
- Battalion Parasol (three)
- Battalion Piesc
- Battalion Zoska (three)
- Battalion Broda 53

Group Chrobry II
- Battalion Lech Zelazny (three)
- Battalion Lech Grzybowski (three)

Group Gurt
- Battalion Gurt (four)
- WSOP Group IV (three)

Group Bartkiewicz (four)

Other units

Battalion Rum (three)
Battalion Kilinski (six)
OW-KB Battalion Jur-Radwari (two)
Company Koszta

POWISLE

Group Krybar
- Battalion Bicz (four)
- Battalion Konrad III (three)
- Group Elektrownia

MOKOTÓW

Regiment Baszta
- Battalion Baltyk
- Battalion Olza
- Battalion Karpaty

Group Grzmaly
- Battalion Krawiec
- Battalion Korwin

Other units

7th Uhlan Regiment Jelen (two)
Artillery Group Granat
1st Squadron Goral
Battalion Odwet II
Battalion Zygmunt (three)
Battalion Oaza
5th WSOP Battalion (two)

PRAGA

Battalion Grunwald

Battalion Bolek

Battalion Olszyna

Battalion Platerowek

OKECIE

7th Infantry Regiment Garluch (Battalions 1, 2, 3 and Artillery
   Company Kuba)

KAMPINOS FOREST

Group Kampinos

   Battalion Korwina

   Battalion Strzaly

   Battalion Znicza

ŻOLIBORZ

Group Zmija (three)

Group Zubr (four)

Group Zaglowiec (one)

Group Zbik

Group Zniwiarz

Group Zyrafa (five)

WOLA

Battalion Sowinski (four) and 18 independent platoons

OCHOTA

Battalions Waclawa (three)

Gustaw (two)

12 independent platoons

GERMAN

Numbers in parenthesis are troop strength listed in German
strength reports.

WEHRMACHT

Oberfeldkommandantur 225, Kommandantur Warschau –
   Generalleutnant Rainer Stahel

Ostpreßen Grenadier-Regiment 4 (894) [1]

Wachregiment 'Warschau' (400) – Oberst Lange

Alarmregiment 'Warschau' (400)

Landesschützen Battalion 996 (650)

Landesschützen Battalion 997 (650)

Landesschützen Battalion 998 (650)

Armee-Panzerjäger-Abteilung 743 (120), 28 Jagdpanzer 38

Panzer-Zerstörer-Bataillon 743, one company

Pioniere-Bataillon 654 (300)

Baupionier-Bataillon 66

Baupionier-Bataillon 146

Baupionier-Bataillon 737

Sicherungs-Bataillon 944 (200)

7. Genesungs-Kompanie (73)

Feldgendarmerie Kompanie 225

Feldgendarmerie Kompanie (mot.) 914

POLICE

Kommandantur Polizei – SS-Brigadeführer Paul Otto Geibel

SS-Polizei-Regiment 22 (800) – Oberst Wilhelm Rodewald

Reserve Polizei Kompanie (220)

SA-Standarte 'Feldherrnalle' (200)

Gendarmerie (250) – Oberst Göde

Ordnungspolizei (150)

Official Bodyguards (300)

Sicherheitspolizei (SD) (150) – SS-Standartenführer Ludwig Hahn

WAFFEN-SS

Kosaken Kompanie (150)

SS replacement battalions (two)

SS-Panzergrenadier Ersatz-Abteilung 3 –
   Obersturmführer Martin Patz

SS- Reitersturm 8 (200) – Haupsturmführer Dichtmann

LUFTWAFFE

Airport security Okecie (800)

Airport security Bielany (500)

Flak-Regiment 80/Flak-Brigade X (3,000)

TOTAL GARRISON: 16,000 men

Luftflotte 6 – General der Flieger Ritter von Greim

Fliegerdivision 1 (HQ at Topolowa)

   1, 4/SG 1, 26 x Ju-87D (at Lobellen, 25km south-south-east
      of Tilsit) [2]

   III/SG 77, 32 x Ju-87D (at Grójec/46km south of Warsaw)

   10.(Pz)/SG 77, 5 x Ju-87D, 11 x Ju-87G (at Kraków)

REINFORCEMENTS IN AUGUST 1944:

SS AND FOREIGN NATIONAL UNITS

SS-Sonderregiment Dirlewanger (881) –
   SS-Standartenführer Oskar Dirlewanger [3]

1st Regiment/Waffen-Sturm-Brigade RONA (Kaminski Brigade)
(1,585) – Sturmbannführer Ivan Frolov

3./SS-Flak-Regiment 'Wiking'

SS-Jäger-Abteilung 501 (461) [4]

Grenadier Kompanie, SS-Junkerschule Treskau

Kampfgruppe der SS-Führerschule Braunschweig

SS-Kompanie (gem.), Warschau

Schwere SS-Kompanie Rontgen-Posen (200) [5]

SS-Kavallerie-Ersatz-Abteilung

III/SS-Polizei-Regiment 17

III/SS- Polizei-Regiment 23

Abwehr-Abteilung D – SD Haupsturmführer Spilker

I and III/ Ostmuselmannische SS-Regiment (550) [6]

Aserbeidschanisches Feld-Bataillon I./111 (657) –
   Hauptmann Werner Scharrenberg

II./Gebirgsjäger-Regiment 'Bergmann' (Azerbaijani) (556) –
   Hauptmann Hubert Mertelsmann [7]

Russische Reiter-Abteilung 580

Reiter-Abteilung 3/Kosaken Sicherungs-Regiment 57 (944)

Kosaken-Abteilung 69 (773)

Kosaken-Abteilung 572 (619)

Kosaken-Abteilung 579

Kosaken-Abteilung 960

Kosaken-Reiter-Rgt. 3 (660)

ARMY UNITS

Pionier-Sturm-Bataillon 500 (604) [8]

Infanterie-Abteilung Arzberger (630) [9]

Grenadier-Abteilung Benthin (545) – Major Benthin [10]

Panzergrenadier-Ersatz-Bataillon 5 (572) [11]

Füsilier-Bataillon 73

Grenadier-Abteilung z.b.V. 550 (400)

Grenadier-Abteilung z.b.V. 560 (400)

Panzerabteilung (Fkl) 302 (160), 24 x StuG III –
   Major Reinert

Sturmgeschütz-Ersatz-Abteilung 200 (160) –
   Major Rupert Gruber [12]

Panzer Sturm-Mörser Kompanie 1000 (56)

Sturmpanzer-Kompanie z.b.V. 218 (78) –
   Hauptmann Kellmann

Panzer Ausbildung Zug 5

Schwere Stellungs-Werfer-Batterie 201 (64)

Artillerie-Abteilung 507 (76), 6 x 105mm l. FH18

Eisb. Panzerzug 75 (49) – Hauptmann Franz Edon

(1 Battery) Schwere Artillerie-Abteilung 154, 4 x 150mm s.FH18

2./ Schwere Artillerie-Abteilung 641, 2 x 305mm mortars

1 Battery of 2 x 210mm Mortars

Heeres Artillerie Batterie 638, 60cm 'Ziu' (113)

Eisb. Artillerie Batterie 686, 38cm 'Siegfried'

Pionier-Sturm-Bataillon 501

Flammenwerfer-Bataillon Krone (326)

Pionier-Sturm-Regiment 'Herzog' – Major Herzog

Heeres-Sturmpionier-Bataillon 46 (614) –
   Major Wollenberg

Pionier-Bataillon 627 (mot.) (737)

Sicherungs-Regiment 608 (618) –
   Oberst Wilhelm Schmidt

Sicherungs-Bataillon 350

POLICE AND MILITIA UNITS

Hilfs. Polizeiabteilung 21 'Sarnow'

Polizeiabteilung 'Burkhardt' (376)

Eisb. Polizei-Kompanie 'Walter' (271)

I/Polizei-Schützen-Regiment 35

Polizei Wach Bataillon 'Warschau' (166)

SD-Kompanie 'Warschau'

SD-Kompanie 'Poznan'

Feuerschütz Polizeiabteilung 96 (mot.) (202)

Polizei Geschütze-Batterie, 4 x 76.2mm Russian guns

Landesschützen-Bataillon 246 (341)

LUFTWAFFE UNITS

Feldersatz-Bataillon (FEB), Fallschirm-Panzer-Division 1
   'Hermann Göring' (800)

REINFORCEMENTS IN SEPTEMBER 1944:

Heeres Artillerie Batterie 428, 60cm Rex, Thor

19. Panzer-Division

   Panzergrenadier-Regiment 73

   Panzergrenadier-Regiment 74

   Panzer-Aufklärungs-Abteilung 19

   Panzer-Artillerie-Regiment 19

   Panzerjäger-Abteilung 19

   Panzer-Pionier-Bataillon 19

   Abteilung 'Schmidt'

   Abteilung 'Bernd'

25. Panzer-Division

   Sturm-Pionier-Bataillon 86

   Panzer-Aufklärungs-Abteilung 25

Fallschirm-Panzer-Division 1 'Hermann Göring'

   I./Fallschirm-Panzergrenadier-Regiment 2 'Hermann Göring'

   I./34. Polizei-Schützen-Regiment – Major Nachtwey

Notes

1 Renamed 1145.Grenadier Regiment on 4 August 1944 and joined 562. Grenadier-
   Division in East Prussia.
2 Four Ju 87 under Oberleutnant Hans-Jürgen Klussmann, stayed in Warsaw and
   operated from Okecie airfield.
3 This unit was upgraded to brigade status in September.
4 Includes three flame-thrower units. Only one officer assigned.
5 Three SMG platoons, one mortar platoon. This unit was formed from SS medical
   X-Ray technicians who had been working in hospitals.
6 Formed from Soviet POWs (Turkestanis, Volga Tatars, Azeris, Kirghiz, Uzbek and
   Tadjiks) in January 1944.
7 This unit was formed by Abwehr's Brandenburgers in late 1941 and the 2./Bataillon
   was formed in 1942. It was composed of Armenian and Georgian volunteers.
8 Stab, two assault companies, one Taifun platoon. Had 60 Goliaths.
9 Originally known as Infanterie Bataillon Reck-Libisch (mixed) but re-named in
   mid-August. Consisted of Stab, three Grenadier companies, one heavy company,
   one anti-tank platoon, one pioneer platoon and one cavalry platoon.
10 Formed from officer cadets in Wehrkreis XXI.
11 Stab, three Grenadier companies, one heavy company.
12 Stationed in Wehrkreis XXI.

OPPOSING PLANS

We wanted to be free and owe this freedom to nobody.
Jan Stanislaw Jankowski, Polish Delegate

POLISH

The AK had begun planning for a national uprising against the Germans as early as 1941, although it was not deemed to be feasible until Germany was near collapse. By November 1943, the AK had developed three main variants of the plan: a general rising across Poland in the event of complete German collapse as in 1918, Operation *Burza* (Tempest) and 'battle for the capital', which envisioned major operations only in Warsaw. Originally, the AK leadership wanted to avoid fighting in cities as that would cause unnecessary civilian casualties and, instead, operate primarily against German lines of communication. Operation *Burza* was intended to allow for decentralized, local actions to assist a Soviet advance into Poland, if the Soviets were willing to cooperate with the AK. Once it became clear in July 1944 that Soviet intentions towards Poland were dishonourable, the AK's planning reverted to the traditional 'Doctrine of Two Enemies' (Germany and Russia) developed by Pilsudski's regime. The main objectives now became to prevent the Germans from levelling Warsaw as they evacuated the city and to prevent the Soviets from installing a Communist puppet regime in the capital. It was

After the assassination of SS-Brigadeführer Kutschera in February 1944, the German security forces greatly increased their level of alertness. The erection of physical barriers and bunkers around their facilities in Warsaw made it difficult for the AK to employ surprise attacks at W-Hour. (Author's collection)

also important for the AK to demonstrate to the world that it was able to participate in the liberation of Poland and not merely wait for Soviet tanks to arrive. Thus, the uprising in Warsaw evolved into an unusual two-headed plan, in which the military objectives were directed against the Germans, but the political objectives were directed against the Soviets.

Bór-Komorowski intended that the uprising would drive out or neutralize the understrength German garrison, then organize a functioning local government prior to the arrival of the Red Army and its odious Lublin Committee collaborators. Jan Jankowski, the delegate from the government-in-exile, demanded that Bór-Komorowski give him at least 12 hours to set up a local government using members of the Underground State. It was also hoped that the RAF could fly in members of the government-in-exile, as well as a company of the Parachute Brigade to add legitimacy to the uprising. With a bit of luck, Stalin would be presented with a fait accompli and Polish independence would have a chance to survive after the war. Even if the Red Army proved hostile to the AK in Warsaw, it would be difficult for them to arrest a 40,000-man army without being noticed by the West. Unlike the Polish officers murdered at Katyn, the AK did not intend to walk meekly into the woods and get a bullet in the back of the head from their NKVD 'liberators'.

The government-in-exile had mixed feelings about the plans for an uprising in Warsaw, with the Polish commander-in-chief feeling that the operation was doomed without Soviet support, while Prime Minister Mikolajczyk favoured making the gamble before Stalin could install a puppet government in Warsaw. As for the timing of the uprising, the government-in-exile left that up to Bór-Komorowski – on the morning of 26 July, the AK received the following radio message from London: 'The Government of the Republic has unanimously resolved to empower you to pronounce the Rising at a time to be determined by you.' Once Soviet tanks were spotted near Praga on 31 July and artillery could be heard in the distance, the AK leadership agreed to implement the uprising on 1 August, setting 'W-Hour' (*wybuch*, 'outbreak') at 1700hrs. Previous resistance planning had envisioned launching an uprising at midnight in order to gain additional surprise, but Bór-Komorowski believed that it would be easier to assemble troops using cover of normal evening 'rush hour' civilian traffic. However, Bór-Komorowski ignored the fact that the German nightly curfew began at 2000hrs and Monter's staff was unable to get the orders out before it was imposed, meaning that the orders actually did not go out until the next morning. This delay meant that less than 20,000 of the 44,000 AK fighters in Warsaw could be assembled in time for W-Hour.

Considering that the AK had spent over two years planning for an uprising, the actual operational plan was more the product of last-minute improvisation rather than meticulous staff work. While it is true that the AK leadership had not intended to fight inside Warsaw, once it became a possible course of action in mid-1944 the failure to coordinate rural partisans with urban insurgents was an incredible omission that should have been addressed in the days leading up to the uprising. It was Bór-Komorowski's function as national commander to activate rural partisans to disrupt German railway lines and road bridges into Warsaw, which would have greatly slowed the German response. Bór-Komorowski also failed to ensure that the dispersed weapons stockpiles from the countryside were gathered prior to the uprising, which greatly handicapped the AK during the critical early days of the rising.

The AK started the uprising with only seven to ten days of food and two to three days of ammunition on hand. Furthermore, the failure to prepare the sewers for covert movement ahead of time – by mapping them out, marking routes and clearing obstructions – indicates a clear failure to prepare for the realities of urban warfare (particularly since the AK had used the sewers to smuggle some weapons into the Warsaw Ghetto in 1943).

Tactically, the planned uprising failed to designate a main effort or primary objectives, which led to failure to secure key terrain such as the Vistula bridges or Okęcie airfield. Bór-Komorowski wanted to capture the Vistula bridges in order to secure easy access into the city for the Red Army and to capture the airfield so that the Allies could fly in military supplies (and possibly members of the government-in-exile), but failed to assign sufficient forces to these tasks. Local commanders were given too much leeway in the objectives and manner of launching the initial attacks, which meant that much of AK's advantage in terms of surprise was wasted in amateurish pinpricks against minor German outposts. Enthusiastic but poorly planned attacks led to heavy losses in the first 24 hours of the uprising. Critical targets such as Generalleutnant Stahel's headquarters in the Bruhl Palace or Gestapo headquarters were too tough for weak neighbourhood AK units to tackle and would have required a well-trained Kedyw unit to have a reasonable chance of a successful attack. After five years of observing the German garrison and thanks to a near-perfect enemy order of battle provided by the Szare Szeregi scouts, the AK should have developed a decent assault plan for each major German position. Furthermore, the AK planned to seize as much of the city as possible and then shift to the defence until the Red Army arrived, but it made no provisions either for a German counterattack or a delay in Soviet arrival.

In fact, the AK's planned uprising was built on dangerous assumptions, made by men who were isolated from the strategic discussions ongoing between the Western Allies and the Soviet Union. Polish plans were based on the delusion that the Red Army – the same Red Army that they knew had not hesitated to disarm the regular Polish Army in 1939 and then murder its captured officers by the thousands – would respect the AK's seizure of Warsaw. Indeed throughout the first weeks of the uprising, Bór-Komorowski and his staff held out the false hope that the Red Army would provide military support to the AK in Warsaw. Finally, the AK leadership did not appreciate the disintegration of support for the Polish cause in Britain and expected an unlikely level of military and diplomatic assistance from the Western Allies.

GERMAN

It was no surprise to the Germans that the AK was planning an uprising in Warsaw, but the Germans failed to anticipate its scale. By mid-1944, the Gestapo had captured thousands of members of the AK, who had been tortured at Pawiak Prison into revealing titbits of information, which were then assembled into a reasonably complete mosaic. The main German method to counter a Polish uprising in Warsaw was to transform all the main German headquarters buildings and barracks in the city into heavily fortified structures that could hold out against local attacks until help could arrive from outside the city. Most German-held buildings had machine-gun bunkers near the entrance, barbed-wire obstacles and roof-mounted sentries. A web of Gestapo informers and street checkpoints were deployed around the city

A number of German units, such as Armee-Panzerjäger-Abteilung 743, were rebuilding in the Warsaw area after being gutted by Operation *Bagration*. The Jagdpanzer 38 (Hetzer) tank destroyers were just arriving in quantity and were dug into camouflaged pits to defend the approaches to the Vistula. (HITM Archives)

to make it difficult for the AK to covertly move arms and personnel around and to provide early warning of an uprising. However, Himmler believed that there would be no Polish uprising and he removed several of the most capable SS units stationed in Warsaw to conduct anti-partisan operations in other areas. Furthermore, the Wehrmacht had not developed a contingency plan to reinforce the garrison, nor had they paid attention to shutting off the city's electrical power and water supplies.

On 27 July 1944, just as the 2nd Tank Army was beginning its drive on Warsaw, Hitler ordered Stahel to transform the city into Festung Warschau and told him to hold the 'Warsaw communications centre with all means and weapons available'. In fact, there were no major defensive lines in existence in the eastern suburb of Praga and Stahel had few troops to man them even if they did. German plans for the defence of Warsaw – against the AK or the Soviets – were hindered by lack of a unified command between the local Wehrmacht, SS and various German civil officials.

Once the uprising began, Hitler wanted to use the Luftwaffe to carpet bomb the city, but Greim quickly informed the OKH that his fuel-starved Luftflotte VI was incapable of accomplishing this mission. Instead, Himmler grabbed at the chance for an independent combat mission for his SS troops and volunteered Bach's anti-partisan command as the perfect instrument to suppress the uprising. Hitler, in a perpetual rage after the attempt on his life two weeks earlier, made it clear that this was no normal military operation. He told the Reichsführer-SS, that 'each inhabitant should be killed, it is not allowed to take any prisoners of war. Warsaw has to be levelled and in this way a terrifying example for the entire Europe is to be created.' Once assigned the mission by Himmler, Bach decided first to establish a cordon around Warsaw to prevent further reinforcements from reaching the city and then use assault *Kampfgruppen* to push through resistance-held areas to relieve the various isolated German garrisons in the city. Once that was accomplished, Bach intended to destroy one city district at a time by massing his firepower and available troops against pieces of the AK. In terms of tactics, the German emphasis in Warsaw was upon firepower, rather than manoeuvre, which allowed a relatively small insurgent force to hold out for such a protracted period.

SOVIET

Through the Soviet Stavka, Stalin issued an order on 27 July for the 2nd Tank Army to attack towards Warsaw, but the original directive did not mention a direct descent on the city. Furthermore, most of the Soviet infantry divisions in the First Belorussian Front were tied up reducing German pockets in places like Brest-Litovsk and Siedlce, so 2nd Tank Army would get no additional infantry reinforcements for city fighting for a week or two. Instead, the 2nd Tank Army's mission appears to have been to establish a bridgehead over the Narew River near Pultusk. With both this and the existing bridgehead over the Vistula at Magnuszew, the First Belorussian Front would have been in a good position to encircle Warsaw in a giant pincer and starve out both the German garrison and the AK. It is unlikely that Rokossovsky wanted to engage in a costly city battle either against the Germans or the Poles, when he had the armour available simply to create another pocket that could be reduced at leisure.

Once the Warsaw Uprising began, the Soviets spent several days trying to figure out what was going on in the city but once it was apparent that the AK had the initiative, Stalin ordered Rokossovsky to suspend all offensive operations around the city. Stalin's initial intent was to wait and see – unsure which side would prevail in the battle for the city. Yet as it became clearer that the Germans were gaining the upper hand, Stalin made the decision to let the Germans destroy the AK. This decision – while denied by pro-Soviet apologists – is clearly evident in both the active Soviet effort to deny airfields to Anglo-American aircraft trying to supply the AK and the failure to provide even modest air or artillery support to the AK once the Red Army occupied Praga in September 1944. Stalin's plans were clearly to let the SS utterly destroy the AK and then to establish his own Polish puppet government in Warsaw as soon as the Germans evacuated the city.

THE BATTLE FOR WARSAW

THE FIRST 96 HOURS

Owing to Bór-Komorowski's mistake in giving the execution order for the uprising just before evening curfew, most of the AK district leaders did not receive the order until the morning of 1 August, giving them only six to eight hours to assemble their troops. Indeed, many personnel did not receive their orders to assemble until just before W-Hour. Once alerted, AK members began to converge on pre-designated assembly points, where they formed into platoons and companies for the first time. Most of the Kedyw units assembled in the cemeteries in the western suburbs of the city, where several stockpiles of weapons had been buried. Weapons were cleaned off, armbands and military insignia were donned and leaders began issuing instructions on the German objectives to be attacked.

Despite Bór-Komorowski's belief that normal civilian traffic would conceal the assembling of the AK, local German patrols were soon aware that something unusual was occurring. The young and brash AK recruits, many carrying weapons for the first time, often acted amateurishly. For example, around 1300hrs several soldiers from Battalion Parasol in Ochota decided to 'frighten' an SS guard post by throwing their Molotov cocktails at it. In Żoliborz, a German patrol spotted a group from the Zywiciel Company

Men of the Battalion Piesc ('Fist') assemble in the Evangelical Cemetery in Wola just before W-Hour. Most of the Kedyw units mobilized in the city suburbs and were thus not available for the initial attacks on German installations in the city centre. (Author's collection)

in the street with weapons around 1350hrs, precipitating a firefight. The SS-Polizei called for reinforcements and the arrival of a few armoured cars succeeded in dispersing Group Zyrafa (Giraffe). Although the AK troops in Żoliborz were fairly well equipped – about 45 per cent were armed – they were so disrupted by prompt German countermoves that they were combat-ineffective even before W-Hour. Seeing reinforced patrols deployed on key street intersections near the German-held Citadel and the Citadel Bridge, the AK attacks on these targets were aborted. Soon, more contacts with armed resistance members were reported in Czerniaków, Mokotów and the city centre. By 1600hrs, SS-Brigadeführer Geibel had received enough reports from his police units to know that the AK was coming out of hiding and he put his SS-Polizei and SD units on full alert. Geibel's 5,000 SS-Polizei and other security troops hunkered down around Gestapo headquarters, the Bruhl Palace and several fortified barracks and waited for the AK to make the next move.

Before W-Hour, Bór-Komorowski and his staff moved to the Kammler Factory in the Wola district, in order to set up their headquarters. Although the Kammler Factory was a well-built structure and guarded by a dedicated AK security platoon, it proved to be a poor choice as a headquarters since it was located very close to an SS-Polizei barracks. By chance, the SS-Polizei spotted armed Polish workmen at the Kammler Factory around 1615hrs and a gun battle erupted. The SS quickly surrounded the building and poured machine-gun fire into it, which knocked out the radio used to communicate with London. For three hours, Bór-Komorowski and much of his staff were pinned down and in danger of capture, until a Kedyw unit finally arrived to drive off the SS-Polizei.

Many of the enthusiastic AK soldiers, eager to strike back at the hated occupiers after five years of oppression, simply did not wait until 1700hrs and began attacking targets of opportunity ahead of schedule. The uprising thus began as a sputtering series of small-scale attacks rather than as a coordinated assault upon German centres of power in Warsaw. By the time

AK troops in Praga on 1 August 1944. Weapons include wz.28 automatic rifles and German MG15 machine guns. Despite the initial exuberance, the AK uprising in Praga was extinguished in less than four days. (Nik Cornish)

39

The first 96 hours of the uprising, 1–4 August 1944

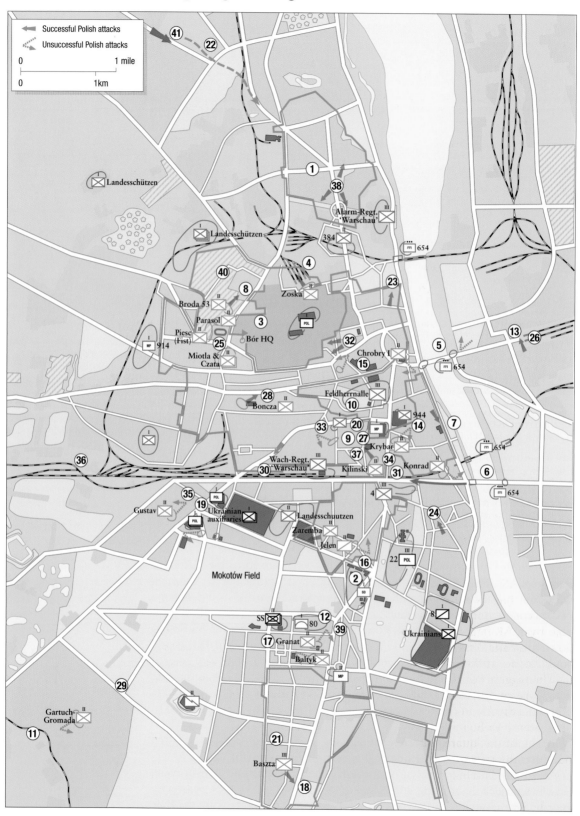

1 August

1. 1350hrs: one of the first premature clashes occurs in Żoliborz. Many of the AK troops in Żoliborz abandon the district and retreat into the nearby woods.
2. 1600hrs: SS-Brigadeführer Geibel places his SS-Polizei and security forces on full alert.
3. 1615hrs: Bór-Komorowski and his staff establish their headquarters in the Kammler Factory but local SS-Polizei detect them and a firefight begins.
4. 1700hrs: AK units begin attacks at W-hour. In one of the first attacks, Battalion Zoska captures the Umschlagplatz rail loading dock and the SS warehouse on Stawki Street.
5. 1700hrs: the AK mounts an attack on the Kierbedzia Bridge with the 103rd Company from Praga and an AK battalion from the Royal Castle, but the attack is repulsed with heavy losses.
6. 1700hrs: Battalion Konrad attacks the Poniatowski Bridge but is repulsed.
7. 1710hrs: AK units attack the German garrison in the electrical power plant and overrun part of the facility, but the last Germans do not surrender until 1200hrs the next day.
8. 1730hrs: Kedyw units capture the St Kinga School on Okopowa Street.
9. 1730hrs: Monter and his staff are established in the Victoria Hotel on Jasna Street.
10. 1730hrs: Stahel, secure inside the Bruhl Palace, informs Hitler about the uprising.
11. The Gartuch-Gromada unit attacks Okecie Airfield and loses 120 men.
12. Company Granat attacks the Flakkaserne and loses 100 of its 120 men.
13. AK forces in Praga succeed in capturing the railway head office on Targowa Street, but most AK units are alerted too late to join in the W-Hour attacks and by the time that they are ready, the German forces in Praga are on full alert.
14. Group Krybar attacks the German garrison in Warsaw University, but is repulsed.
15. AK troops fail to capture the bank on Bielanksa Street. However, Stahel evacuates the small German garrison on the night of 3 August and the AK occupies the building the next morning.
16. The Jelen unit attacks the Gestapo Headquarters and is slaughtered.
17. Regiment Baszta's Battalion Baltyk attacks the SS-Polizei Barracks on Narbutta Street and is repulsed with 30 per cent losses.
18. The remainder of Regiment Baszta seizes the Krolikarnia Palace.
19. Evening: the AK attack against the SS-Polizei barracks on Narutowicz Square in Ochota fails, thereby preventing a link-up with the city centre. The AK district commander retreats with most of his troops into the woods to the south, leaving only 300 troops to hold two redoubts controlling Aleja Grojecka.
20. 2000hrs: Battalion Kilinski captures the 16-storey Prudential Building near Napoleon Square, the tallest building in Warsaw.
21. Evening: AK forces consolidate in southern Mokotów, but many troops retreat south into the woods.

2 August

22. Dawn: AK troops in Żoliborz launch an unsuccessful attack on Bielany airfield.
23. The AK captures the State Securities (PWPW) Building and most of the Old Town.
24. The AK occupies the Social Securities (ZUS) Building and consolidates its position in Czerniaków.
25. 0800hrs: Battalion Zoska captures two Panther tanks in Wola.
26. Midday: the AK units' holding positions in the Praga rail yard are defeated and the uprising in this district collapses prematurely.
27. 1700hrs: Battalion Kilinski captures the main post office.

3 August

28. Battalion Chrobry I captures the Nordwache police station in the city centre.
29. The lead elements of the RONA Kaminski Brigade arrive on the outskirts of Ochota.
30. AK units seize the Postal railway station and part of the Polytechnic Institute.
31. The Germans send a few tanks from the 19. Panzer-Division across the Poniatowski Bridge towards the main railway station but they encounter numerous barricades and ambushes and make little progress.
32. Polish troops in the Old Town extend their area of control by occupying the Blank Palace, the Arsenal and the Mostowski Palace.
33. Night: Battalion Kilinski fights its way into the lower floor of the German bastion in the PAST telephone exchange but cannot hold the position.
34. Polish troops and civilians succeed in erecting two barricades across Nowy Swiat that blocks this thoroughfare to German traffic.

4 August

35. Two Tiger tanks sent into Ochota are knocked out by Kedyw anti-tank teams.
36. Kampfgruppe Dirlewanger arrives on the outskirts of Wola.
37. 1400hrs: the first Stuka attack on insurgent positions near the main post office.
38. AK troops expand their control in Żoliborz between Wilson Square and Inwalidow Square.
39. The Germans begin counterinsurgency operations in Mokotów, murdering 200 people in the area of Olesińska Street.
40. Night: first airdrop received of 12 arms containers from the RAF in Italy (in western suburbs).
41. German attacks on outskirts of Żoliborz force AK to abandon worker housing area.

that most AK units turned out in force at W-Hour, the Germans were waiting with their fingers poised on the triggers of their MG42 machine guns, safe behind concrete and sandbags. Rushing out from buildings located near their objectives, AK fighters were usually met by a hail of gunfire that quickly shut down most attacks. Other AK units, such as Battalion Odwet II in Mokotów, could not act at W-Hour since they had only token amounts of weapons.

The biggest Polish successes on the first day were achieved in the Old Town, the city centre and Wola. There were few German troops in the Old Town and the AK troops were able to seize several large buildings, such as the State Securities building (PWPW), which were used to anchor the defence. Near Napoleon Square, Battalion Kilinski captured the 16-storey Prudential Building, the tallest in Warsaw, at 2000hrs. Elements of Battalion Zoska captured the Umschlagplatz rail loading dock and a nearby SS warehouse on Stawki Street. Stanislaw Likiernik, who was part of the attack, said that 'At exactly 5 p.m. we jumped over the fence at the back of the stores. We shot

The Poniatowski Bridge over the Vistula on 30 August 1944. Although unable to seize the bridge, AK forces remained within sight of the bridge for nearly a month. (Warsaw Uprising Museum, MPW-IP/1165)

several SS men dead. ... A young SS officer who survived our initial assault had built a barricade of packing cases on the first floor. He must have amassed a large amount of ammunition, as he kept us under almost constant fire.'[4] Eventually, the Kedyw troops were able to eliminate this German officer with hand grenades and seize the warehouse, which contained a large number of SS camouflage smocks as well as tons of flour, sugar and cereals. The Kedyw troops quickly donned the captured SS smocks and the captured food stocks were distributed to civilians.

In Powisle district, along the Vistula, the AK had recruited 23 employees of the electrical power plant and these men had snuck weapons and explosives into the facility. Geibel reinforced the German garrison at the plant to 100 SS-Polizei, but they were unaware of the AK presence inside. At 1710hrs, the AK soldiers led by Kapitan Stanisław Skibniewski (Cubryna) detonated explosives under one of the main buildings to stun the Germans and they quickly isolated them in a few barricaded areas of the plant. By noon the next day, the AK had secured the power plant after suffering 17 killed and 27 wounded. German losses were 20 killed and 78 captured. The seizure of the power plant provided electricity to Warsaw for a month and kept the AK's weapons factories operational.

Since the AK leadership hoped to fly in reinforcements and supplies from London, the AK attempted to seize both Okecie and Bielany airfields. Okecie Airfield was defended by 800 Luftwaffe troops, equipped with 20mm flak guns. Hopelessly outnumbered and outgunned, the 7th Infantry Regiment Garluch attacked Okecie Airfield and lost 120 men. An attack on Bielany also failed. The Granat Company attacked the Flakkaserne of the Luftwaffe's Flak-Regiment 80 south of the city and lost over 100 of its 120 men in the failed assault. In nearby Ochota district, the 800 AK troops failed to seize the SS-Polizei barracks in Narutowicz Square and were unable to establish a direct link with other resistance-held areas in the city centre. As night fell, the district AK commander decided to take most of his troops into the woods to the south, leaving only about 300 troops in two redoubts on Kaliska Street and Wawelska Street.

4 Norman Davies, *Rising '44*, pp. 250.

Monter tried to decapitate the German leadership in Warsaw with attacks on their main headquarters in the police district west of Lazienki Park, but the attacking forces were far too weak to succeed. There were two SS replacement battalions with over 1,400 troops in the Stauferhaserne on Rakowiecka Street, as well as five Tiger, one Panther and four PzKpfw IV tanks from the Wiking and Totenkopf divisions. The Jelen unit shelled Gestapo headquarters with a couple of home-made mortars, which forced Geibel to seek shelter in the basement, but when the Polish assault groups left cover to assault the building they were virtually wiped out by automatic weapons fire. Regiment Baszta, one of the best units in the AK, was committed to seize the SS-Polizei Barracks on Narbutta Street, but its Battalion Baltyk suffered nearly 30 per cent losses when it attacked the well-fortified SS troops. The Germans also succeeded in holding all three telephone exchanges in Warsaw, which greatly hindered Monter's command and control by preventing him from using the still-functional phone system. Many of the German facilities in Warsaw were put under siege, but the AK lacked the strength to reduce them.

However, the biggest Polish failure on the first day was the inability to seize any of the bridges over the Vistula River. Oberleutnant Karl Eymer's 2. Kompanie of Pioniere-Bataillon 654 had just finished placing demolition charges on the four Vistula River bridges when the uprising began. Eymer had a 27-man platoon stationed on the Kierbedzia Bridge and a 29-man platoon on the Poniatowski Bridge. Much of the Polish plan for seizing the four Vistula bridges rested with the 6,500 AK troops in Praga, but these had been among the last to receive word of the uprising and were the least ready for action at W-Hour. Podpułkownik Antoni Żurowski (Huber), in charge of the AK troops in Praga, was able only to mount weak attacks on the Kierbedzia and Poniatowski bridges. The 103rd AK company attacked the east end of the Kierbedzia Bridge at 1700hrs while Battalion Boncza,

Polish civilians began constructing barricades on all the major streets on the second day of the uprising. Much of the battle revolved around German efforts to break through the barricades and Polish efforts to defend and rebuild them. (Author's collection)

43

assembling in the ruins of the Royal Castle, attempted to attack the west side of the bridge. Żurowski's men had to cross open ground to get on the bridge approaches and they were quickly spotted by the German pioneers, who had sentries mounted in the twin towers at each end. The German pioneers laid down a heavy barrage of MG42 machine-gun fire on the exposed Polish troops, hitting many and driving the others back under cover. Although Żurowski's troops had some automatic rifles, they could not hit the German defenders, who were under cover. The 103rd Company lost 42 men and the battalion attacking from the Royal Castle was also pushed back with heavy losses, ending the chances for the AK to capture either bridge. Further south, Battalion Konrad attacked the east side of the Poniatowski Bridge but was also beaten back with heavy losses. Not only were Żurowski's men unable to accomplish their primary mission of seizing the Vistula River bridges, but their uprising in Praga was quickly crushed. By chance, the Fallschirm-Panzer-Division 1 'Hermann Göring's second Panzer battalion and other units detraining in Praga's Eastern train station were pressed into action against the local insurgents. After suffering heavy losses and seeing a strong display of German military might at the outset, most of the AK troops in Praga decided either to go back under cover or to leave the city.

From the beginning of the uprising, the AK soldiers were joined by thousands of Polish civilians, who helped to build street barricades and round up isolated Germans. However, Polish efforts to construct effective barricades were hindered by German rooftop snipers and machine-gun teams, who made moving around on open streets very dangerous. Individual German armoured vehicles moved up and down Aleje Jerozolimskie, machine-gunning anything that moved. By the end of the first day, as the sun set at 2044hrs, the AK had achieved virtually none of its objectives in Warsaw. Although AK units had seized substantial chunks of the Old Town, Sródmiescie (city centre) and the Wola suburbs, few areas were really secure or linked together. AK units in Mokotów were isolated and the units in Żoliborz opted to leave the city and

regroup in the Kampinos Forest. Those buildings that had been captured were useful for building Polish morale, but contributed little to victory. Furthermore, Polish command and control on the first day was awful, with Bór-Komorowski out of contact at W-Hour and Monter's headquarters unable to communicate with any of its subordinate units.

Secure inside the Bruhl Palace, Stahel informed Hitler at 1730hrs about the beginning of the uprising, but early reports were sketchy. As more information came in, indicating a citywide uprising, Stahel demanded reinforcements from Vormann's 9. AOK, but there were few reserves available. Vormann was able to scrape up Sicherungs-Regiment 608, Eisb. Panzerzug 75 and the 800-man replacement battalion from the Fallschirm-Panzer-Division 1 'Hermann Göring' to reinforce key points around Warsaw, but he had no forces available for serious counterattacks. After watching the Luftwaffe and the Heer prove unable or unwilling to crush the revolt, Hitler turned to Himmler and the SS to suppress the Warsaw Uprising. Early on 2 August, Bach was appointed commander of the SS forces operating against Warsaw. Reinefarth was ordered to round up several SS units in Posen and proceed directly to Wola. Dirlewanger and Kaminski's RONA were also ordered to send strong *Kampfgruppen* to Warsaw.

On the first day of the uprising it was estimated that the AK suffered about 2,000 casualties – about 10 per cent of the force it committed. Stahel estimated that he had lost 500–600 men on the first day. German material captured by the AK included six howitzers, seven mortars, two anti-tank guns, 27 Panzerfäuste, 13 heavy and 57 light machine guns, 373 rifles and 103 pistols. While the amount of ammunition captured was not large, the additional machine guns greatly increased Polish defensive capabilities.

It began raining on the evening of 1 August and scattered showers continued the next day. Around 0900hrs, Bór-Komorowski was able to re-establish radio contact with London and informed the government-in-exile of the uprising. During the night, Monter had used couriers to reorganize his

LEFT
A blocking detachment of Polish soldiers from the elite Battalion Zoska stand watch near the Gesiówka prison camp on 5 August 1944. (US Holocaust Museum, 80908)

RIGHT
The Prudential Building as seen from Napoleon Square on 17 August 1944. The building has already received a direct hit from artillery, but has not burned yet. By the end of the battle, the building would be a twisted wreck of concrete and steel. (Warsaw Uprising Museum, MPW-IN/2996)

scattered forces and ordered them to continue attacks. In contrast, Stahel did little to help his numerous encircled garrisons and was content to await help from outside the city. The rest of Old Town was liberated on the second day of the uprising and Battalion Kilinski, led by former cavalry officer Kapitan Henryk Roycewicz (Leliwa) managed to capture the main post office by 1700hrs. The Germans lost 23 killed and 57 captured, as well as large quantities of weapons. Two German armoured cars and a Hetzer tank destroyer were damaged by Molotov cocktails and captured; the Hetzer was incorporated into a street barricade near the post office. However, a renewed attack on Bielany Airfield was also driven off.

The elite Kedyw units under Pułkownik Jan Mazurkiewicz (Radoslaw) actually played relatively little role in the first days of the uprising, since most of the battalions were positioned around Bór's headquarters in the north-west suburbs of the city. On the other hand, the Kedyw units did not suffer heavy losses at W-Hour and had over 24 hours to assemble in relative peace. On the morning of 2 August, local SS commanders ordered several Panther tanks from I/Panzer-Regiment 27, 19. Panzer-Division, that had been under repair in western Warsaw to break through the Polish barricades in Wola and clear a way to the Bruhl Palace. With negligible infantry support, these tanks advanced blindly into the Kedyw stronghold along Okopowa Street. Around 0800hrs, two Panthers attacked the barricade on Karolkowa Street, which was defended by the 2nd Company of Battalion Zoska. These Kedyw troops were equipped with captured Panzerfäuste as well as British-supplied PIAT anti-tank launchers, Gammon grenades and improvised explosives. One Panther was hit on the turret by either a PIAT or Panzerfäuste and the crew panicked when they realized that the Poles had anti-tank weapons. Meanwhile, the second Panther was attacked with Molotov cocktails and a lucky hit on the vision slit blinded the driver. Both crews abandoned their vehicles and were captured. Battalion Zoska now had two relatively intact Panther tanks, which were quickly pressed into service flying Polish colours.

Already frustrated by the scale and audacity of the Polish attacks, the SS began to make reprisals against Polish civilians. Geibel ordered the execution of all 600 Polish prisoners in the holding cells of Gestapo headquarters and an SS-Polizei unit murdered dozens of civilians with hand grenades at a nearby Jesuit seminary. Outside Warsaw, Himmler gave orders for Generał brygady Rowecki to be executed at Sachsenhausen concentration camp.

By the third day of the uprising, Polish attacks were beginning to taper off because of dwindling ammunition supplies. Small groups of AL and NSZ fighters joined the AK in the uprising and Monter now had perhaps 30,000 fighters, although the weapons situation was still abysmal. The only major successes for the resistance on 3 August was the capture of the Nordwache police station in the central Sródmiescie district by Battalion Chrobry I (Valiant) and the occupation of the abandoned National Bank. The Germans were able to push a few tanks from 19. Panzer-Division down the main Aleje Jerozolimskie from the Poniatowski Bridge, but their advance was hindered by frequent ambushes and obstacles. With plenty of labour available and only limited German activity, the Poles spent much of the day improving their barricades to deny the use of the main roads to German armour.

Meanwhile, German reinforcements from Posen were detraining at Blonie, 23km west of Warsaw, and moving towards the city. On 4 August, the lead elements of Einsatzgruppe Gruppenführer Reinefarth began to arrive on the edge of Wola and Ochota, but since he had only 1,000 troops with him Reinefarth decided to wait until the next day before launching a major attack. However, Reinefarth's troops did begin rounding up and executing Polish civilians in the suburbs, in accordance with Hitler's orders. Oddly, a local German commander decided to test the defences in Ochota by sending two Tiger I tanks retained from 3. SS-Panzer-Division 'Totenkopf' to probe the

Polish AK officers interrogating Major Max Dirske on 18 August 1944. Unlike the Germans, the Poles treated all but SS captives according to the Geneva Convention. SS prisoners were usually summarily executed. (Warsaw Uprising Museum, MPW-IN/2224)

barricades. Once again, the Kedyw units demonstrated the futility of sending tanks into an urban area without infantry support – one Tiger was knocked out with a Panzerfaust and the other was abandoned after a near miss. However, the Luftwaffe also made its first appearance over Warsaw since the uprising began, using a few Stukas to bomb the area around the post office in the city centre around 1400hrs. Recognizing that a German counterattack was imminent, Monter ordered the AK units in Warsaw to revert to the defence in order to conserve ammunition, although the siege of buildings such as the PAST telephone exchange continued. That night, the resistance received its first drop of supplies from the Polish squadron in Brindisi, which delivered 12 containers with PIATs and light machine guns. In Wola, Pułkownik Mazurkiewicz had grouped about 1,600 men from his Kedyw units into Group Radoslaw to defend the area with his best troops and weapons, but his left flank in Ochota was only lightly defended. After several days of tangling with isolated police units, the AK would now have to face the fury of organized German counterattacks, supported by armour and Stukas.

GUDERIAN'S COUNTERATTACK, 1–5 AUGUST

The German counterattack against the Soviet 2nd Tank Army near Radzymin began at 0600hrs on 1 August – 11 hours before the Warsaw Uprising began. Guderian's intent was to use General von Saucken's XXXIX Panzer Korps in Praga and the newly formed IV SS-Panzer Korps under SS-Obergruppenführer Gille to launch a pincer attack between Wolomin and Sulezowsk to cut off the Soviet 3rd Tank Corps. While Guderian's plan called for four Panzer divisions, only parts of the Fallschirm-Panzer-Division 1 'Hermann Göring' and 5. SS-Panzer-Division 'Wiking' were in place by the morning of 1 August. Guderian ordered Vormann to begin the attack anyway, with the 4. and 19. Panzer divisions joining the counterattack over the next few days. The 2nd Tank Army shifted to the defensive just before Guderian's counterattack

German infantry fighting their way towards the Saxon Gardens on 6–7 August 1944. The soldier in the street is overwatching while the rest of his squad dashes across the street. (HITM Archives)

Dispositions around Warsaw, 2400hrs 31 July 1944

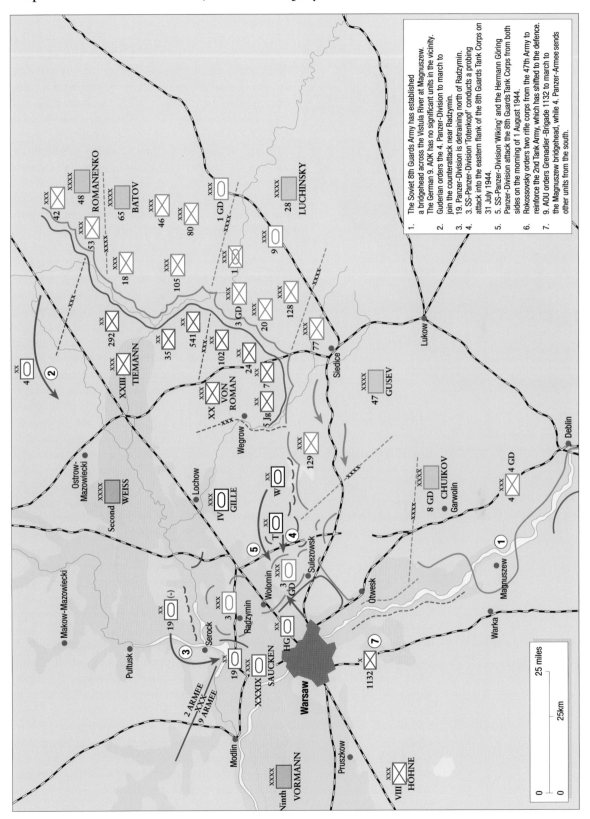

1. The Soviet 8th Guards Army has established a bridgehead across the Vistula River at Magnuszew. The German 9. AOK has no significant units in the vicinity.
2. Guderian orders the 4. Panzer-Division to march to join the counterattack near Radzymin.
3. 19. Panzer-Division is detraining north of Radzymin.
4. SS-Panzer-Division 'Totenkopf' conducts a probing attack into the eastern flank of the 8th Guards Tank Corps on 31 July 1944.
5. SS-Panzer-Division 'Wiking' and the Hermann Göring Panzer-Division attack the 8th Guards Tank Corps from both sides on the morning of 1 August 1944.
6. Rokossovsky orders two rifle corps from the 47th Army to reinforce the 2nd Tank Army, which has shifted to the defence.
7. AOU orders Grenadier-Brigade 1132 to march to the Magnuszew bridgehead, while 4. Panzer-Armee sends other units from the south.

49

began, but its three corps were spread out and had little infantry support. Fallschirm-Panzer-Division 1 'Hermann Göring' attacked the 8th Guard Tanks Corps from the west with a regiment, while 'Wiking' struck it from the east with 17 Jagdpanzer IV tank destroyers. Given the small scale of the German attacking forces, only seven Soviet tanks were destroyed on the first day of the counterattack and no ground was lost. Furthermore, the diversion of part of 'Herman Göring's Panzer regiment and 'Wiking's reconnaissance battalion to deal with the uprising in Praga further weakened the German counterattack.

Parts of 4. and 19. Panzer divisions began reaching the front north of Wolomin on 2 August, but only Wiking made any attacks that day. Rainy weather during 1–4 August further hindered the German deployment schedule. It was not until 3 August that Guderian had the bulk of his four Panzer divisions in place, with about 174 tanks and assault guns, to mount a serious counterattack. However, by this time the 2nd Tank Army had reinforced its defences to the extent that a pincer attack was no longer practical and Guderian had to settle for a concentric attack on the 3rd Tank Corps' salient around Wolomin. In two days of heavy fighting, the Germans destroyed about 100 Soviet

Polish troops in the Old Town in August. Note the fairly uniform appearance of the troops and that many are carrying German stick grenades. (Warsaw Uprising Museum, MPW-IN/715)

tanks and pushed the 3rd Tank Corps out of Wolomin, but once it became clear that this battle would not result in a major operational triumph, Guderian called off the counterattack on 5 August. Soviet strength in this sector was now increasing, with the arrival of two rifle corps to reinforce the 2nd Tank Army. Instead, Guderian opted to leave 4. Panzer-Division and 73. Infanterie-Division to defend Praga, while the 'Hermann Göring' and 19. Panzer-divisions were sent south to counterattack the Magnuszew bridgehead.

Although Stalin claimed that Guderian's counterattack had thrown the Red Army back '200 kilometres' and inflicted heavy losses, this was a deliberate lie. The 2nd Tank Army lost 116 of its 679 remaining tanks and assault guns during 1–6 August and its 3rd Tank Corps had been pushed back 20km, but the bulk of its combat power was still intact. Personnel losses were only 2,200 out of an initial strength of about 35,000 troops. Guderian's counterattack had not even affected the 16th Tank Corps, which still held its position seven kilometres south-east of Praga. Guderian's counterattack had failed to harm the Soviet armoured spearhead seriously or to push it back from Warsaw. Nevertheless, on 7 August Stalin ordered the Stavka to withdraw the 2nd Tank Army from the Warsaw front and to redeploy it to the south, leaving only infantry divisions to observe the Germans in Praga. Even if fuel shortages had suspended the Soviet tank drive on Warsaw, Soviet artillery and air power could have been used to support the AK if directed by Stalin. Instead, the unsuccessful German counterattack at Wolomin was used as an excuse to do nothing to help the insurgents in Warsaw for over one month, indicating that Soviet actions were driven more by political than military considerations.

THE WOLA MASSACRE, 5–6 AUGUST

By the morning of 5 August, Reinefarth had assembled almost 5,000 troops in the suburbs adjacent to Wola and Ochota and he intended to punch a hole through the thin Polish crust defences in order to clear a route to link up with Stahel's trapped forces in the Bruhl Palace. However, Reinefarth was not a trained tactician and he made the beginner's mistake of splitting his limited forces into four uncoordinated assault groups and tried to launch a broad front assault moving from west to east. He did benefit from some limited air support and a few tanks and assault guns on loan from 9. AOK, but his units were a hotchpotch of officer cadets, Luftwaffe, SS-Polizei, Azerbaijanis, Russians and German convicts. Reinefarth also employed a number of *Volksdeutsche* who lived in the Wola area to inform him about the location of AK defences. Meanwhile, Monter and Radoslaw had poorly deployed the best AK troops in this area, with five Kedyw battalions defending the area around Bór-Komorowski's headquarters, but only weak local units to hold the southern approaches in Wola and Ochota. Thousands of AK troops were available a few miles away in the city centre, but poor communications made it almost impossible for Monter to shift any to Wola to help stem the German onslaught.

At 0800hrs, Reinefarth's attack began with Luftwaffe aircraft dropping incendiary bombs on Wola, setting many houses alight. Then Oberst Schmidt's Sicherungs-Regiment 608 stepped off on the left, moving towards the Jewish Cemetery and the Kammler Factory. In the centre, a 500-man police group formed from three motorized police companies advanced into Wola on the north side of Wolska Street. On the right, Dirlewanger advanced on the south side of Wolska Street with his two battalions and an attached Azerbaijani battalion moving parallel on side streets. Most Wehrmacht regular units were held back in reserve, since this was to be an SS-run 'special action'. The 1,700-man RONA *Kampfgruppe* under Major Yuri Frolov was also supposed to attack Ochota at the same time, but this undisciplined unit

The Wehrmacht sent every available soldier from its training units in Posen to form Kampfgruppe Reck. Although heavily armed, these young recruits were only partly trained and unready for urban combat. (HITM Archives)

German counterattack in Wola and Ochota, 5–6 August 1944

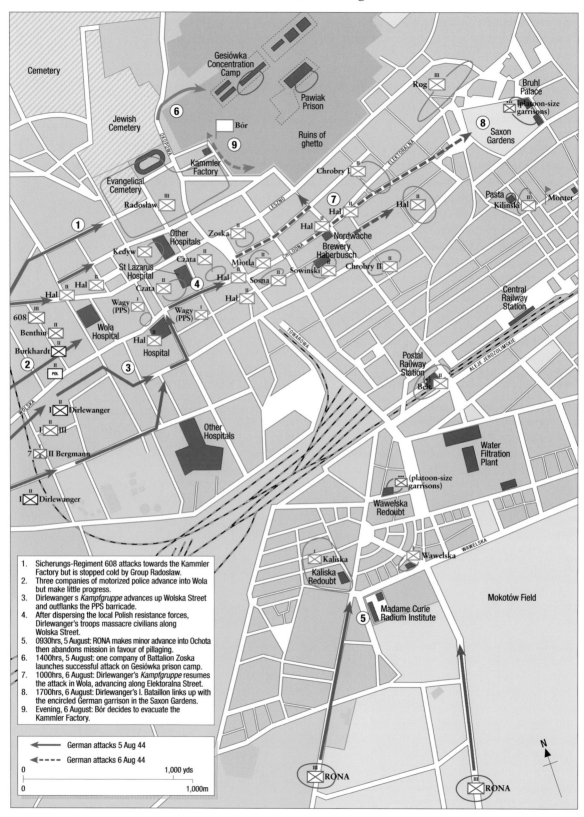

Cemetery

Gesiówka
Concentration
Camp

Pawiak
Prison

Rog

Bruhl
Palace
(platoon-size
garrisons)

Jewish
Cemetery

6

Bór

9

Ruins of
ghetto

8

Saxon
Gardens

Kammler
Factory

Chrobry I

Pasta
Kilinski

Monter

Evangelical
Cemetery

Radoslaw

Hal

Hal

7

Hal

Zoska

Other
Hospitals

1

Kedyw

Czata

Miotla

Nordwache
Brewery
Haberbusch

Central
Railway
Station

St Lazarus
Hospital

Hal

Sosna

Sowinski

Chrobry II

Czata

4

Hal

Hal

Hal

Wagy
(PPS)

Wagy
(PPS)

608

Benthin

Wola
Hospital

Hal

Burkhardt

Hospital

2

POL

3

Postal
Railway
Station

Belt

I Dirlewanger

I III

Other
Hospitals

Water
Filtration
Plant

7 II Bergmann

(platoon-size
garrisons)

I Dirlewanger

Wawelska
Redoubt

Kaliska

Wawelska

Mokotów Field

Kaliska
Redoubt

Madame Curie
Radium Institute

5

1. Sicherungs-Regiment 608 attacks towards the Kammler
   Factory but is stopped cold by Group Radoslaw.
2. Three companies of motorized police advance into Wola
   but make little progress.
3. Dirlewanger s *Kampfgruppe* advances up Wolska Street
   and outflanks the PPS barricade.
4. After dispersing the local Polish resistance forces,
   Dirlewanger's troops massacre civilians along
   Wolska Street.
5. 0930hrs, 5 August: RONA makes minor advance into Ochota
   then abandons mission in favour of pillaging.
6. 1400hrs, 5 August: one company of Battalion Zoska
   launches successful attack on Gesiówka prison camp.
7. 1000hrs, 6 August: Dirlewanger's *Kampfgruppe* resumes
   the attack in Wola, advancing along Elektoralna Street.
8. 1700hrs, 6 August: Dirlewanger's I. Bataillon links up with
   the encircled German garrison in the Saxon Gardens.
9. Evening, 6 August: Bór decides to evacuate the
   Kammler Factory.

German attacks 5 Aug 44

German attacks 6 Aug 44

0   1,000 yds

0   1,000m

N

RONA

RONA

did not join in the attack for two more hours. Radoslaw's Kedyw troops near the Jewish Cemetery badly shot up Schmidt's security troops and forced them to retreat to their starting positions. Nor did the police group do much better. However, Dirlewanger's troops were able to advance 2,500m up Wolska Street before they encountered the first barricade, which was defended by a poorly armed Polska Partia Socjalistyczna (Polish Socialist Party, PPS) platoon. The SS troops easily bypassed the barricade by using a side street then attacked the defenders from behind, scattering them. While Polish sniper fire caused police units to move very cautiously, Dirlewanger was oblivious to losses among his own troops and advanced with great relish.

Dirlewanger had been personally ordered by Himmler to use terror to break the morale of the insurgents and the suburbs of Wola were his object lesson. SS troops went from door to door, rousting out all civilians and then setting the buildings afire. No one was exempt – Dirlewanger's troops rounded up every man, woman and child along a one-kilometre stretch of Wolska Street. Many civilians were shot on the spot, but there were so many that Reinefarth ordered them sent to the rear for execution since they were getting in the way of the military mission of pushing towards Stahel. Thousands of civilians were herded westwards, where they were executed in the yard of the Ursus Factory. Watching these columns of civilians, Reinefarth lamented that, 'this is our biggest problem. These refugees! I don't have enough ammunition to kill them all!' Dirlewanger's troops then went on a rampage through the hospitals in Wola, murdering 500 staff and patients at the Wola Hospital on Plocka Street and 600 at St Lazarus' Hospital.

In Ochota, Frolov's RONA unit finally began advancing around 0930hrs. Despite the fact that it had armour support and there were fewer than 300 lightly armed Poles in this sector, Frolov's unit barely advanced 300m on 5 August. Instead, the RONA troops spent most of their effort looting, getting drunk, murdering civilians and raping Polish women. The RONA troops did not even bother attacking the AK-held Kaliska and Wawelska redoubts in Ochota, which blocked access to the Aleje Jerozolimskie. Instead, their main accomplishment of the day was murdering most of the staff and patients at the Maria Curie Sklodowska Radium Institute. Andrzej Ulankiewicz, part of a platoon from Battalion Parasol defending the Wawelska redoubt said, 'We witnessed people being doused with gasoline and burned alive in the park of the Radium Institute at Wawelska Street. We realized that we must fight to the very end because otherwise we would all be killed without mercy by this vicious band of thugs.' Many of the Wehrmacht troops assigned to support the Kaminski Brigade were disgusted with the non-military behaviour of this unit and some regular units refused to work with it.

While Dirlewanger was rampaging through Wola, Radoslaw made a foolish decision to commit some of its best Kedyw troops to a secondary attack in a quiet sector. Around 1400hrs, Kapitan Waclaw Micuta (Wacek) led a company of Battalion Zoska and one of the precious captured Panther tanks in an attack on the Gesiówka prison camp in the former Jewish ghetto. After the Panther destroyed the guard towers with 75mm gunfire, the Zoska troops were able to penetrate the defences and eliminate the Sicherheitspolizei camp guards at a cost of only one killed and five wounded. A total of 324 men and 24 women prisoners were liberated in the camp, including survivors of the Jewish ZOB resistance group from 1943. Although this attack boosted Polish morale, it occurred while the SS was massacring over 10,000 Polish civilians only 1,400m to the south-west.

Bach arrived outside Wola around 1700hrs on 5 August and assumed command of the entire operation. During the course of 5–6 August, Reinefarth's troops murdered between 30,000 and 40,000 civilians in Wola – exceeding the total of 33,771 Jews killed at Babi Yar outside Kiev in two days in September 1941. The Wola Massacre was the worst single battlefield atrocity committed in Europe in World War II, but it did not produce the effect that Hitler had intended. Instead of terrorizing the population, the indiscriminate murder of thousands of civilians drove the rest of the population into full-hearted support of the AK. Surrender now meant annihilation, so the defenders were encouraged to mount a fanatical defence. After a few days of watching the SS slaughter civilians in Wola and Ochota, Bach realized that the 'no prisoners' policy was counterproductive and stiffening resistance so he ordered a change in policy. From here on, Bach ordered that women and children could be spared (and sent to concentration camps) but most able-bodied males would still be executed. Although Bach emphasized his moderating influence to spare his neck at Nuremburg, the fact is that German troops continued to murder large numbers of Polish civilians in Warsaw. However, Bach directed that about 20,000 survivors of the massacres in Wola and Ochota be sent to a camp in Pruszków, west of the city.

Meanwhile, Monter's headquarters at the Victoria Hotel was slow to grasp the situation developing in Wola but by the evening it was recognized that the AK defences in the West were hard-pressed. Bór-Komorowski decided to re-locate his headquarters from the Kammler Factory – now in danger of being cut off by German advances – to the relatively secure Old Town. Monter decided to divide the city up into three main 'battle centres': Sródmiescie, South and North.

The Germans resumed their drive in Wola at 1000hrs on 6 August. The AK battalions Parasol and Zoska repositioned some of their units to attempt to block Dirlewanger from advancing further into the city, but it was not enough. AK troops along Wolska, Chlodna and Elektoralna streets succeeded in disabling several German armoured vehicles with PIATs and Molotov cocktails, but Dirlewanger's troops began to use captured Polish civilians as human shields in front of their vehicles, which enabled them to get past some ambushes. Dirlewanger made his attack down Elektoralna Street, straight through the defences of battalions Chrobry I and Hal. By 1700hrs, Dirlewanger's advanced units had reached the trapped German garrison in the Saxon Gardens. The next morning, in a fit of bravado, Reinefarth personally made a dash in an assault gun up Elektoralna Street under fire in order to link up with Stahel in the Bruhl Palace. Shortly thereafter, Stahel returned with Reinefarth to Wola, effectively handing over his remaining authority to the SS. The Germans now had a tenuous corridor through the city centre to some of their embattled garrisons, but they lacked the infantry to secure the entire route. Instead, armoured vehicles were used to make high-speed supply runs down the semi-cleared route, dodging ambushes and barricades.

WOLA AND OCHOTA ARE LOST, 6–11 AUGUST

As the Polish resistance lost its grip on the outer suburbs in Wola and Ochota, the insurgents were compressed into four main areas: Żoliborz, the Old Town, the city centre and Mokotów/Czerniaków. The AK also had a strong presence in the Kampinos Forest in the north and the Germans had been unable to isolate the city completely, so some personnel and supplies were trickling in from the outside. The Warsaw Uprising began to enter a new phase on 8 August, as it became clear to the Germans that they would have to reduce each section of the city in turn, with a series of deliberate attacks. Bach decided to finish mopping up Wola and adjacent areas in order to solidify the German hold over their thin corridor to the Bruhl Palace, then move in and crush the main resistance centre in the Old Town. Dirlewanger's *Kampfgruppe*, reinforced with 14 Hetzers and two Azerbaijani battalions, was ordered to consolidate the area around the Bruhl Palace and then continue all the way to Kierbedzia Bridge in order to restore German control over the Vistula crossings. Meanwhile, the Kaminski Brigade under Major Frolov was left to terrorize Ochota district, but Bach realized that the unit was incapable of conducting real city fighting. The next wave of German attacks would be spearheaded by Kampfgruppe Schmidt from the north and Kampfgruppe Reck from the west.

Oberst Schmidt's group consisted of his own Sicherungs-Regiment 608, a heavy machine-gun platoon, a company of Panzer pioneers, a battery of l.FH18 howitzers, as well as support from Eisb. Panzerzug 75. Major Reck, just arrived from the infantry school at Posen, was given two battalions of raw infantry recruits, a company of Azerbaijanis, an engineer platoon and a battery of Nebelwerfer. Both of these assault groups were very weak in reliable infantry and fire support and the only general support asset available was Panzerabteilung (Fkl) 302 with 23 StuG III assault guns and 36 radio-controlled demolition vehicles. Reinefarth, still in tactical control of the city battle, kept his less reliable Cossack and police units in reserve.

Schmidt's troops entered the former ghetto from the north and encountered only light resistance, since there were no civilians in this devastated area and only a few Kedyw detachments. While some of his troops cleared the ghetto ruins, the bulk of his forces pivoted east and began attacking the west side of the Old Town but after two days of fighting their advance was brought to a halt. At the same time, Reck's troops mounted a major effort to clear the

WOLA MASSACRE, 1030HRS, 5 AUGUST 1944 (pp. 56–57)

Both Adolf Hitler and Reichsführer Heinrich Himmler ordered the SS to use terror to crush the Warsaw Uprising as quickly as possible. On the morning of 5 August, the Germans began attacking into Wola, the western suburb of Warsaw, spearheaded by the troops of SS-Oberführer Oskar Dirlewanger. These were no ordinary Waffen-SS troops, but a special anti-partisan unit formed from former convicts and military misfits. After the small number of AK troops in this part of Wola had been eliminated, Dirlewanger **(1)** ordered his troops to use squad-sized assault groups to smash in the doors of each house with axes and crowbars **(2)** and then drag out all the inhabitants. Civilians who resisted were shot on the spot or even thrown out of upper-storey windows **(3)**. Groups of civilians were executed in alleyways by Dirlewanger's men with

small arms fire **(4)**. Soon, Wolska Street was littered with the corpses of several thousand civilians, most with bullet holes in their heads **(5)**. Dirlewanger's men took no prisoners for the first three days in Warsaw and murdered men, women and children indiscriminately. Many female prisoners, like these Polish nurses **(6)** from the Wola Hospital, were first raped then murdered. Dirlewanger's men were also authorized to loot from their victims and the houses, before setting the buildings alight with hand grenades or flame-throwers **(7)**. Although not directly involved in most of the slaughter of civilians, the German Army did provide support units to Dirlewanger, such as this StuG III **(8)** from Sturmgeschütz-Ersatz-Abteilung 200. Within two days, the Germans had murdered well over 30,000 civilians in Wola – the worst massacre in Europe in World War II.

Kedyw units out of the Jewish Cemetery and the north-west corner of Wola around the Kammler Factory. Radoslaw's troops fought tenaciously for this area since it was one of the designated areas for Allied airdrops, but ultimately it was a misuse of some of the AK's best troops to defend a non-critical area. Supported by Leutnant Klussmann's Stukas and his Nebelwerfer, Reck's forces pounded the area into rubble and inflicted significant casualties upon the Kedyw units. One of the captured Panther tanks was repeatedly hit by German anti-tank fire and had to be abandoned. By the time that Radoslaw decided to withdraw his troops before they were entirely encircled, Schmidt's units had cut their escape route across the ghetto. Battalions Zoska, Miotla and Wacek finally managed to leave Wola on 11 August just before the German noose closed and escape across the ghetto in small groups towards the Old Town, but the Kedyw units were badly depleted in this pointless fighting. The last captured Panther tank led the Kedyw units along Stawki Street towards the west until it was immobilized by a hit from a German anti-tank gun; the Kedyw troops set it on fire and continued their retreat.

In Ochota, the two small AK units were not as hard pressed at the units in Wola and they were quick to sense the lax behaviour of the RONA troops operating in their district. When a large group of RONA troops were spotted looting several buildings in plain view of an AK-held strongpoint, the local AK commander decided to mount a counterattack. The RONA troops were caught completely by surprise and their commander, Major Frolov, was killed by a flame-thrower. After witnessing countless atrocities committed by these men, the Polish troops took no prisoners and annihilated a company-sized element of RONA. In less than a week of fighting, the Kaminski Brigade had lost over 500 of its 1,700 troops and accomplished nothing of military value. Eventually, the Germans brought up some pioneers to reduce the Wawelska and Kaliska redoubts. On 11 August, both buildings were attacked with Goliath demolition vehicles and the AK troops hurriedly evacuated their redoubts through connecting tunnels that had been dug to nearby sewer canals. Some troops succeeded in reaching the city centre, but at least two groups were eliminated in the sewers by German troops.

Two soldiers from the NSZ Company Ziuk on Wieiskiej Street. Note that one soldier is holding a US-made M3 sub-machine gun. (Warsaw Uprising Museum, MPW-IN/3501)

THE OLD TOWN, 8–19 AUGUST

Once Wola and the ghetto were cleared of major AK units, Reinefarth reorganized Reck's and Schmidt's forces for an immediate attack on the Old Town from the west. In the Old Town and New Town, Podpułkownik Karol Ziemski (Wachnowski) had between 5,500 and 7,000 resistance troops, who proved to be more than a match for the 3,000 attacking German troops. Radoslaw's Kedyw troops, having escaped from Wola, formed the core of the resistance in this area. Indeed, Wachnowski's troops were full of fight and they even made an unsuccessful sortie on 9 August to try and destroy Eisb. Panzerzug 75 near Gdansk Station.[5] Bór-Komorowski had shifted his headquarters to the Old Town and his signal unit had set up radio station Błyskawica (Lightning), which improved morale among the 100,000 civilians crowded into this district. While the Polish situation was serious, the Germans' conquest of Wola and Ochota had succeeded only in compressing the resistance forces into smaller areas that were now easier to defend. German commanders were also quick to note that Polish resistance was increasing – almost certainly a result of the massacres committed in Wola and Ochota. The Poles began to make use of Warsaw's extensive sewer system on 6 August and a telephone line was laid through the sewers to connect Monter's headquarters in the city centre with Bór's headquarters in the Old Town.

Dirlewanger's troops launched probing attacks on 9 August and managed to capture the ruins of the Royal Castle, but they were not yet strong enough to advance further. Although Bach was eager to clear out the Old Town to remove the threat to the nearby Vistula bridges, Reinefarth was unable to gather enough troops to mount a major attack on the Old Town until 11 August. That morning, Dirlewanger launched an attack towards the southern end of the Old Town from the ruins of the Royal Castle with two battalions of Azerbaijani troops, supported by three StuG III assault guns and some Hetzer tank destroyers. However, when the German armoured vehicles approached the major barricades leading into the Old Town, they were showered with dozens of Molotov cocktails and Filipinka grenades. When their armoured support retreated, the German infantry was decimated by sniper fire. On 12 August, Dirlewanger tried again and was again driven off. Indeed, the AK troops were able to mount a counterattack that succeeded in capturing five machine guns, 30 anti-tank mines and 11,600 rounds of ammunition. Goliath and B IV demolition vehicles were used to blast apart several insurgent barricades and heavily defended houses, but the Poles had sufficient manpower to quickly rebuild them each night. AK fighters quickly learned to neutralize the Goliath by breaking its trailing control wires with hand grenades. Major Reck's *Kampfgruppe* joined the attack on 12 August, attacking out of the east end of the ghetto towards the Krasinski Gardens. Reck's troops, mostly green infantry replacements and with few trained officers and NCOs, lacked the skill for close-quarter fighting and they suffered accordingly when they tried to advance into the heavily built-up Old Town. Polish snipers proved particularly adept at engaging the Germans from well-concealed locations, which took a heavy toll on officers and NCOs.

Reinefarth's attack continued on 13 August, but after three days it had made no real progress. Around 1800hrs, three German StuG III assault guns attacked the barricade on Podwale Street, near Zamkowy Square and the

---

5 The Germans referred to this as Danzig Station.

Royal Castle. After shelling the barricade, the StuGs retreated and a B IV demolition vehicle was sent to blast the obstacle. Unlike the remote-control Goliath, the B IV had to be driven close to its target then detonated remotely. When troops from Battalion Gustav fired on the approaching vehicle, the German driver abandoned it and ran back to his lines. Elated at capturing what they thought was a light tank, the men from Battalion Gustav drove the vehicle back towards Bór's headquarters on Kilinski Street to show it to their commander. Upon arriving there, hundreds of soldiers and civilians swarmed around the vehicle to view their trophy. At 1900hrs, the 500kg charge on the vehicle detonated, killing about 100 soldiers from Battalion Konrad, 20 from Battalion Wigry and perhaps 200 civilians. Body parts were plastered all over the exterior of the buildings on Kilinski Street. Bór himself, who was approaching to see the vehicle, suffered a concussion.

Dirlewanger's *Kampfgruppe*, reinforced with five 20mm anti-aircraft guns and pioneer teams with eight flame-throwers, made another attack on the barricades blocking access into the Old Town on 16 August, but was again repulsed. Wachnowski used the brief lull in German attacks to mount several counterattacks, designed to improve land communications with the city centre. Battalion Wigry caught Kampfgruppe Reck off guard and succeeded in recapturing the Mostowski Palace, while battalions Chrobry I, Czata 49 and Zoska were less successful. By the end of 16 August, Oberst Schmidt's troops were beginning to probe the north end of the New Town, meaning that this would now be a three-front fight.

Reinefarth had almost nothing to show for a week of attacks upon the Old Town. German armoured vehicles were unable to operate effectively in this restricted area and the Poles were able to knock out several vehicles with PIAT anti-tank launchers and Molotov cocktails. German casualties in street fighting had proved heavy – often 25–30 per cent of units – and Bach realized that he could not satisfy Hitler's demand to crush the uprising quickly with these forces and tactics. Unable to defeat the AK quickly, Bach and Reinefarth decided to burn the Old Town to the ground. On 17–18 August, Stukas bombed the area around the Old Town's market square, setting numerous fires. Meanwhile, Schmidt shelled the northern section of the Old Town with a battery of light field howitzers and Eisb. Panzerzug 75. However, the bombardment failed to dent the Polish defence and follow-up attacks by

Reck and Schmidt's troops were repulsed. Some of Reck's infantry did gain a foothold in the Krasinski Gardens, but Battalion Czata 49 successfully defended the Warsaw Arsenal. While Polish losses in the Old Town were serious, after more than a week of heavy fighting, the AK defence in this area remained intact.

LONDON AND MOSCOW, AUGUST 1944

The British Government was never keen on supporting an uprising by the AK because of apprehension about causing irreparable harm to Anglo-Soviet relations. In particular, the British Foreign Ministry was incensed by the refusal of the Polish Government-in-exile to accept Stalin's territorial demands in eastern Poland after the war, which Winston Churchill had already conceded at the Tehran Conference. Churchill was sympathetic to Poland, but saw the Red Army as more critical to the defeat of Germany than the AK. Thus, when the government-in-exile requested that the British release the Polish Parachute Brigade for service in Poland and bomb German military bases around Warsaw, it was refused out of hand. British military leaders informed the government-in-exile that Warsaw was too far away from Allied bases to provide effective support.

Once the Warsaw Uprising began, the British Government viewed it with a great deal of indifference. The government-in-exile did gain permission to use the Polish Flight 1586 in Brindisi for a renewed airdrop effort, but the first mission on the night of 4 August was disappointing. It took the Polish-piloted Halifax bombers up to six hours to fly from Brindisi to Warsaw, carrying less than four tons of supplies each, and even dropping their cargo from 90m only 12 containers landed in Polish-held drop zones. Royal Air Force leaders were quick to use aircraft losses en route to claim that the mission was too costly and would be feasible only if Stalin granted refuelling rights at nearby Soviet bases in the Ukraine, but the British request on 20 August was denied. Instead, throughout August the RAF kept up a minimal air supply effort to Warsaw that succeeded only in delivering token amounts of weapons and supplies.

Oddly, most histories of the uprising fail to note that the RAF made two large-scale bomber raids on the port of Königsberg on the nights of 26 and 29 August. Each raid involved over 170 Lancaster bombers delivering 2.5 tons of bombs each, against a target that did not support the Allied advance on the Western Front or have any critical German industries. The distance from RAF bases in Lincolnshire to Königsberg was 1,354km, which was 74km less than the distance to Warsaw. These two raids demonstrate that the RAF did have the ability to operate in strength over central Poland and had RAF Bomber Command been used to conduct re-supply missions over Warsaw instead of attacking pointless secondary targets, the AK might have received enough arms to blunt the German attacks.

Stalin had been well aware that a Polish uprising was likely and this was confirmed by Polish Prime Minister Mikolajczyk, who was in Moscow in late July, on a futile mission to try and patch up Polish–Soviet relations. Despite having called for the Poles to revolt, as soon as indications of fighting in Warsaw were detected, Stalin ordered Rokossovsky to halt his advances towards the city. Stalin's approach to the Warsaw Uprising was based on standard communist 'deny–minimize–ignore' tactics. Initially, Stalin disputed Mikolajczyk's claim that an uprising had begun and for a few days, Soviet propaganda said there was no uprising. Once the AK began regular

German pioneers preparing a Goliath demolition vehicle for an attack on a Polish barricade. The Goliath could carry a 75kg charge that was powerful enough to demolish reinforced concrete structures, but its control wires were vulnerable to damage and the vehicle was rather slow, with a top speed of only 10km/h. (Bundesarchiv, 101III-Ahrens-026-12)

radio broadcasts from the city – clearly refuting Soviet propaganda – Stalin switched to minimizing the uprising, claiming that only a 'handful of criminals' were involved. Gradually, Stalin shifted to ignoring the uprising: Allied requests to permit air resupply missions were refused and attempts by the AK to establish contact with Rokossovsky's forces went unanswered. Soviet operations around Warsaw were suspended until the Germans had crushed the AK. It was clear that Stalin had no intention of helping the insurgents – whom he labelled 'enemies of the Soviet Union' – because they could hinder his plan to install a puppet communist government in Warsaw.

THE OLD TOWN, 20 AUGUST–2 SEPTEMBER

Although Wachnowski's and Radoslaw's troops had repulsed numerous German attacks on the Old Town, the German bombardment steadily crushed the morale of the 40,000 Polish civilians huddling in their basements. Most people had joined the uprising expecting a short fight, followed by the arrival of either Soviet tanks or Polish paratroopers from England, but after two weeks it was becoming apparent that help was not coming. The Germans had also belatedly cut off the city's water supply, which made it difficult to care for the hundreds of wounded and almost impossible to fight the numerous fires. The Old Town was rapidly becoming a pile of shattered rubble, with about half the buildings destroyed, although the Germans had captured surprisingly little ground. Wachnowski still had some 4,000 troops left, although Radoslaw's Kedyw troops had suffered about 70 per cent casualties.

At this point, Monter made one of his few efforts to coordinate a multi-battalion attack in order to relieve the pressure on the Old Town. The AK still had significant numbers of troops in the city centre and the northern suburb of Żoliborz, so Monter ordered them to gather sufficient forces to mount a pincer attack from both the north and the south to break through to the Old Town. The troops from Żoliborz, reinforced by 650 partisans from the Kampinos Forest, were the main effort and they attempted a night attack on the Gdansk railway station. However, the Germans were expecting this

DEFENCE OF THE PIWNA STREET BARRICADE, 24 AUGUST 1944 (pp. 64–65)

One of the most potent weapons wielded by the AK was the simple street barricade, which greatly restricted the movement of German armoured vehicles. Hundreds of barricades were built in Warsaw after 1 August and much of the tactical combat revolved around German efforts to capture or destroy barricades at key intersections and Polish efforts to prevent this. The fighting around the barricades leading into the southern section of the Old Town were particularly fierce and Dirlewanger's SS troops in Zamkowy Square made repeated attacks upon the barricade at Piwna Street that led directly to the Old Town's market square. The AK's Battalion Wigry defended this barricade. Piwna Street was only three metres wide at its entrance – too narrow for German tanks to move through – and the Poles built the barricades far enough down the street that the German infantry would have to move down a narrow funnel, with three-storey buildings on both sides.

In this scene, Dirlewanger has sent forward a platoon from the Aserbeidschanisches Feld-Bataillon I./111, who were attached to his command, supported by an SS flame-thrower team and a StuG III assault gun. The 75mm rounds from the StuG III have not seriously damaged the barricade (1) and as the Azerbaijani troops attempt to scramble atop the barricade, they are met by a fusillade of Polish small arms fire and grenades (2) that decimates the lead squad. Polish snipers firing from concealed positions in the wrecked upper floors of the buildings (3) pick off the German NCOs and the flame-thrower team (4). Several Molotov cocktails, hurled by catapult-type devices, have even set the StuG III alight (5). Each repulsed German attack left behind weapons and ammunition that were quickly recovered by the AK. The fight for the Piwna Street barricade went on for over two weeks and the SS troops never succeeded in breaking through before the AK evacuated the Old Town.

move and the lightly armed AK forces were no match in open fighting. Once detected, the Germans launched flares and opened fire with mortars and heavy machine guns, pinning the troops from Żoliborz in the open. Eisenbahn Panzerzug 75 added its fire as well. The Polish attack on the night of 21 August was repulsed with over 400 casualties. Wachnowski also tried to create a corridor through the area around Teatralny Square, but his troops only succeeded in recovering some ground near the Town Hall. Reinefarth responded to these Polish failures with a renewed series of attacks from each direction, but they were poorly coordinated and the Germans were stretched so thinly that they could not commit more than a battalion against any single objective. Dirlewanger's piecemeal attacks were stopped cold, with considerable losses. Reck's troops also failed to seize a critical barricade, but his troops set the Warsaw Arsenal on fire, forcing Battalion Chrobry I to abandon it and retreat to Dluga Street. The next day, Schmidt's troops attacked the massive Polish Security Printing Works (PWPW) on Sanguszki Street but could not gain entry. Ignoring Monter's orders not to waste ammunition on German aircraft, a Polish heavy machine gun stationed at the Town Hall succeeded in shooting down a Stuka on 23 August.

Despite the German failure to break through the main Polish barricades and seize key terrain in the Old Town, both Bór and Wachnowski realized that the increasing loss of civilian life and urban destruction was rapidly becoming intolerable. Finally, they decided to evacuate the Old Town as soon as practical. Bór and his staff left the Old Town on the night of 25 August, using the underground sewers to escape to the city centre. Although the Poles had been using the sewers routinely since early in the battle, the Germans proved surprisingly inept at stopping this underground traffic. German pioneers did make some use of the Taifun – a new fuel-air explosive weapon that pumped gas into the sewers then detonated it – but not enough to seriously disrupt Polish underground communications. The Germans also routinely dropped hand grenades down manhole covers whenever they detected sounds, but this was insufficient to prevent the movement of thousands of AK personnel underground. Once Bór and his staff were established in the city centre – where conditions were still relatively normal – he continued efforts to assist the Old Town's defence. Several attempts were

A group of soldiers from Battalion Chrobry II guarding the barricade at Siennej and Wielkiej streets. Note that they are primarily armed with pistols, so they could not engage German forces at a distance. (Warsaw Uprising Museum, MPW-IN/3722)

made to break through the German ring around the Old Town to evacuate the wounded or get in supplies, but all were repulsed.

The linchpin of the Polish defence in the Old Town was the four-storey PWPW Building, whose thick concrete walls were impervious to all but heavy artillery fire. Group Lesnik held this structure along with members of Group Radoslaw. Radoslaw, although wounded, commanded this section of the Old Town's defence. Eisenbahn Panzerzug 75 bombarded the PWPW Building for several days, which collapsed part of the building but failed to drive out the defenders. On 23 August, Schmidt's troops attacked the PWPW from two sides, but failed to make any progress in three days of fighting. At the same time, Schmidt sent other troops to push slowly down Bonifraterska Street to the west of the PWPW building, threatening to cut off the defenders.

By late August, Korpsgruppe von dem Bach was beginning to receive some significant reinforcements, including Panzerabteilung (Fkl) 302, a company of Sturmpanzer IVs, two Sturmtigers, the 600mm mortar 'Ziu', more pioneers and Flammenwerfer-Bataillon Krone. These units were committed to reinforce Schmidt's and Reck's ongoing attacks on the Old Town and began to tip the battle in the Germans' favour. On 27 August, Schmidt sent 1,600 troops, supported by assault guns, against the 200-odd Polish defenders in the PWPW Building. In a fight reminiscent of the grain elevator at Stalingrad, the Germans slowly fought their way into the massive building. By 0830hrs on 28 August, the Germans had broken resistance in the building and Schmidt's men proceeded to murder the Polish wounded huddled in the basement. The loss of the PWPW Building shattered the AK defences in the northern part of the Old Town and, for the first time, Schmidt's forces easily occupied a large section on 29 August. Meanwhile, Dirlewanger's troops had fought their way into the southern section of the Old Town but were stopped in fierce fighting around St John's Church, which had been blown to pieces by a Goliath. Despite the increased firepower, German casualties were mounting rapidly; by 28 August, Reinefarth's troops had suffered over 3,800 casualties out of an attacking force of 13,400 men – a 28 per cent casualty rate.

Using PIATs supplied by Allied airdrops, Group Radoslaw disabled three StuG III assault guns in the Old Town. However, Radoslaw's troops had reached their limit and only 1,500 able-bodied troops remained in the Old Town. Ammunition stocks were also nearly exhausted. With the defence wavering, Wachnowski decided to evacuate his best troops, including Battalion

Czata 49, to the city centre on 30 August. Since most of the wounded and civilians could not use the sewer system, Wachnowski intended to use his evacuated units to attack in conjunction with Monter's forces to make one last effort to create a corridor between the Old Town and the city centre. Spearheaded by Battalion Czata 49, the AK troops began their attack at 0300hrs on 31 August and they succeeded in reaching the area of Teatralny Square before the attack broke down. Realizing that the Polish defence was weakening, Reinefarth stepped up his attacks on the Old Town on 1 September, pressing in from all four sides. Battalion Chrobry I made a valiant last stand for a while on Dluga Street, but then its members took to the sewers at 2000hrs and escaped to the city centre. Altogether, about 4,500 AK troops succeeded in escaping from the Old Town through the 1,700m-long sewer route and they even managed to bring 100 German POWs with them. The German failure to anticipate or prevent this escape was one of their greatest mistakes of the battle. One particularly daring Pole, Kapitan Bialous Ryszard (Jerzy), commander of Battalion Zoska, led 80 of his men dressed in captured SS camouflage smocks through enemy lines to the city centre. However, there was no escape for the 2,500 wounded AK troops and 35,000 civilians left in the Old Town. When Reinefarth's troops advanced into the ruins of the Old Town on the morning of 2 September, they shot about 7,000 captives, while the remainder was sent to Mauthausen and Sachsenhausen concentration camps.

As a postscript to the liquidation of the Polish resistance in the Old Town, Bach ordered Dirlewanger to eliminate the remaining AK enclaves along the Vistula River. The sub-district of Powisle, which included the vital electrical power plant, had been relatively quiet for most of August. Groups Krybar and Rog had about 1,000 troops to defend this area. Dirlewanger began his attack on Powisle on the morning of 3 September, supported by artillery and Stuka attacks. The power plant was finally demolished by direct fire from an 88mm flak gun on 4 September. Initially, Group Rog repulsed the German attacks on the northern part of Powisle but at the cost of weakening its defences in the south. On 5 September, the Germans attacked the narrow corridor across Nowy Swiat Avenue, connecting Powisle to the Old Town, and rapidly overran this area. With their link to the city centre nearly severed,

BELOW LEFT
The PAST telephone exchange on fire. Polish troops had the trapped German garrison inside under siege for nearly three weeks. (Author's collection)

BELOW RIGHT
German troops surrendering to Battalion Kilinski after the successful AK attack on the PAST building on 20 August. A total of 157 Germans were captured in the building, as well as stocks of weapons. (Warsaw Uprising Museum, MPW-IN/668)

ABOVE LEFT
A German B IV demolition
vehicle moving in front of a
Sturmpanzer (left) and a StuG III
assault gun (right) on a Warsaw
street. (Author's collection)

ABOVE RIGHT
A soldier from Battalion KB
Sokol at the barricade on
Brackiej Street. He is armed
with a British Sten, but wearing
a pre-war Polish helmet.
(Warsaw Uprising Museum,
MPW-IN/1404)

the Polish troops in Powisle opted to evacuate the district. However, the Germans launched a powerful concentric attack before the evacuation was completed and Group Rog's troops fought a ferocious rearguard action to enable as many of the civilians and wounded to escape as possible. By nightfall on 6 September, Reinefarth's troops occupied all of Powisle.

THE CITY CENTRE AND THE SOUTHERN SUBURBS, 8 AUGUST–2 SEPTEMBER

While the Old Town was being flattened, life in the city centre was almost normal for the first few weeks of August. Bach and Reinefarth lacked the resources to mount serious attacks against this area or the southern suburbs as long as the fight in the Old Town dragged on, so they were content to blockade these areas and harass them with occasional bombing. Monter had perhaps 5,000 armed troops in the city centre, as well as about 2,000 in Mokotów and 1,200 in Czerniaków. However, Monter's plan to link the southern districts with the city centre had been constantly thwarted by Geibel's heavily fortified SS-Polizei areas around Lazienki Park and Rakowiecka Street and could only communicate with the suburbs via the sewers. Despite these tactical failures, one of the AK's greatest successes was in capturing several large food warehouses that enabled a city of nearly one million to hold out for two months of siege warfare.

Generalmajor Günter Rohr arrived on 10 August to take over the hotchpotch of German forces operating in the southern districts of Mokotów and Czerniaków. After hearing about the drunken misbehaviour of the Kaminski Brigade in Ochota, Vormann decided to send a professional army officer to restore military discipline. Rohr immediately demanded that the Kaminski Brigade be withdrawn and even Bach and Reinefarth agreed that it had no military value, so it was sent to the ruins of Wola to guard civilian evacuees. Instead, the RONA troops proceeded to murder and rape the evacuees, which greatly reduced the number of civilians willing to accept German guarantees and leave the city. When Kaminski proved unwilling to stop the misbehaviour of his troops, Bach finally conceded that the RONA troops were more of a liability than an asset and decided to remove them from the battle. On 28 August, Kaminski was invited to an SS conference at Lodz, but en route he was arrested and executed by the Gestapo. Bach then sent the RONA troops to the Kampinos Forest to strengthen the cordon around Żoliborz, but the Polish partisans in the forest made short work of

A Polish insurgent armed with a PIAT anti-tank launcher. Radoslaw's troops received several timely airdrops of PIATs that greatly strengthened their defence of the Old Town. (Author's collection)

these misfits. A company-sized partisan force attacked the Kaminski Brigade near the village of Truskaw at midnight on 2 September, killing 91 of the RONA troops and capturing most of their weapons. The surviving RONA troops ran off in panic into the woods and Bach quietly sent the unit away.

Rohr had few units to mount a serious attack against Warsaw's southern suburbs, but 9. AOK gave him a company of Hetzer tank destroyers, some flak units and Pionier-Bataillon 627 (mot.), while Geibel provided a battalion of SS-Polizei and two battalions of *Landesschützen*. Rohr's troops were able to seize the water filtration plant from Battalion Chrobry II on 12 August, but they were unable to advance further north. Kampfgruppe Reck did launch probing attacks into northern Sródmiescie on 15–17 August, but also failed to make any substantial progress. Reinefarth moved schwere Stellungs-Werfer-Batterie 201 with six Nebelwerfer 42/43 launchers into the Saxon Gardens, where they proceeded to lob rockets into the area around Napoleon Square on 15 August.

German Nebelwerfer rockets launched from a fixed battery located near the Saxon Gardens. This battery was able to fire both high-explosive and incendiary rockets in concentrated volleys that could shatter the upper floors of civilian buildings and start serious fires. (Bundesarchiv, 101I-696-426-15)

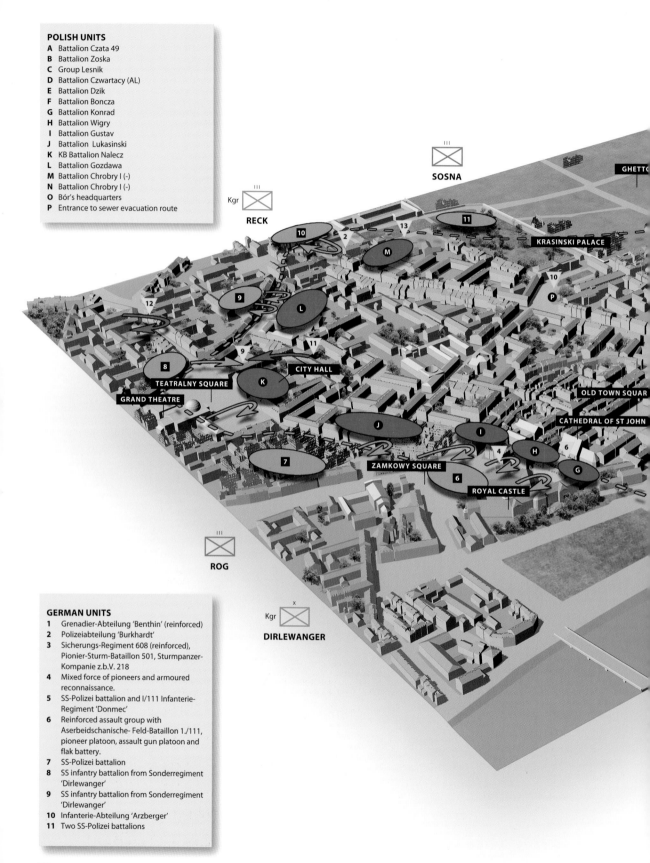

POLISH UNITS

A Battalion Czata 49
B Battalion Zoska
C Group Lesnik
D Battalion Czwartacy (AL)
E Battalion Dzik
F Battalion Boncza
G Battalion Konrad
H Battalion Wigry
I Battalion Gustav
J Battalion Lukasinski
K KB Battalion Nalecz
L Battalion Gozdawa
M Battalion Chrobry I (-)
N Battalion Chrobry I (-)
O Bór's headquarters
P Entrance to sewer evacuation route

SOSNA

GHETTO

Kgr RECK

KRASINSKI PALACE

P

CITY HALL

TEATRALNY SQUARE

GRAND THEATRE

OLD TOWN SQUAR

CATHEDRAL OF ST JOHN

ZAMKOWY SQUARE

ROYAL CASTLE

ROG

Kgr DIRLEWANGER

GERMAN UNITS

1 Grenadier-Abteilung 'Benthin' (reinforced)
2 Polizeiabteilung 'Burkhardt'
3 Sicherungs-Regiment 608 (reinforced),
   Pionier-Sturm-Bataillon 501, Sturmpanzer-
   Kompanie z.b.V. 218
4 Mixed force of pioneers and armoured
   reconnaissance.
5 SS-Polizei battalion and I/111 Infanterie-
   Regiment 'Donmec'
6 Reinforced assault group with
   Aserbeidschanische- Feld-Bataillon 1./111,
   pioneer platoon, assault gun platoon and
   flak battery.
7 SS-Polizei battalion
8 SS infantry battalion from Sonderregiment
   'Dirlewanger'
9 SS infantry battalion from Sonderregiment
   'Dirlewanger'
10 Infanterie-Abteilung 'Arzberger'
11 Two SS-Polizei battalions

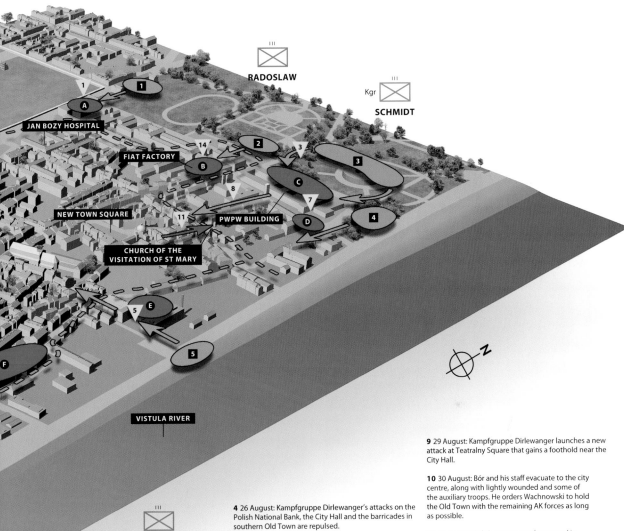

RADOSLAW

Kgr SCHMIDT

JAN BOZY HOSPITAL

FIAT FACTORY

NEW TOWN SQUARE

PWPW BUILDING

CHURCH OF THE
VISITATION OF ST MARY

VISTULA RIVER

N

TRZASKA

EVENTS

1 24 August: Kampfgruppe Schmidt captures part of the ruins of the Jan Bozy Hospital, which weakens the insurgents' northern defensive line in the New Town.

2 24 August: Kampfgruppe Reck attacks Battalion Wigry in the Simonsa Passage on Dluga Street but is repulsed after heavy fighting.

3 25 August: Kampfgruppe Schmidt attempts another attack on the PWPW Building, but is repulsed by Group Lesnik. Other German elements continue the fight for Jan Bozy Hospital and the Fiat Factory.

4 26 August: Kampfgruppe Dirlewanger's attacks on the Polish National Bank, the City Hall and the barricades in southern Old Town are repulsed.

5 26 August: Kampfgruppe Dirlewanger succeeds in capturing the Quebracho tannery, which weakens the insurgent's eastern defences.

6 27 August: Group Rog defeats an attempt by Dirlewanger's troops to blow up their stronghold in St John's Cathedral with Goliath demolition carriers.

7 28 August: Kampfgruppe Schmidt finally succeeds in capturing the PWPW Building after a week of heavy fighting.

8 29 August: Kampfgruppe Schmidt follows up the capture of the PWPW Building with a bold advance into the New Town that succeeds in capturing the insurgent stronghold around the Church of the Visitation of St Mary. However, Schmidt cannot dislodge the Kedyw units in the ruins of the Fiat Factory.

9 29 August: Kampfgruppe Dirlewanger launches a new attack at Teatralny Square that gains a foothold near the City Hall.

10 30 August: Bór and his staff evacuate to the city centre, along with lightly wounded and some of the auxiliary troops. He orders Wachnowski to hold the Old Town with the remaining AK forces as long as possible.

11 30 August: Polish counterattacks succeed in recapturing some of the ground lost on the previous day.

12 31 August: 0300hrs. Wachnowski orders part of Battalion Czata 49 to move through the sewers from the Old Town and to attack Dirlewanger's troops near Teatralny Square from behind, hoping to create a ground corridor for a break out to the city centre. However, the Germans detect the attack and repulse it, inflicting 300 casualties on the AK troops.

13 31 August: the Luftwaffe conducts a concentrated bombing of Battalion Chrobry I's stronghold in the Simonsa Passage and kills 120 AK soldiers.

14 31 August: Kampfgruppe Schmidt finally succeeds in capturing the ruins of the Fiat Factory and the AK defence in the northern sector begins to crumble.

THE FINAL BATTLES FOR WARSAW'S OLD TOWN, 23–30 AUGUST 1944

While the Germans were distracted by Kaminski's antics, Monter tried to use his limited reserves to eliminate some of the remaining isolated German garrisons. The telephone exchange in the 11-storey PAST Building had been encircled by Battalion Kilinski since the beginning of the uprising and its 157-man German garrison was suffering badly from lack of food and water. A few German armoured vehicles had made supply runs to bring food to the trapped troops but morale was crumbling. Several Germans committed suicide and the commander radioed Rohr that they could not hold out much longer. On 19 August, Rohr mounted a relief effort towards the PAST Building by attacking the nearby Polish-held Warsaw Polytechnic. Battalion Golski defended the stout university buildings. The Germans attacked with six assault guns and Goliaths but only gained a foothold in the campus area. Finally, after fighting all day, Battalion Golski – which had suffered 25 killed

The southern entrance to Piwna Street off Zamkowy Square in 2007. Note the narrowness of the street – barely three metres wide at the entrance – which meant that Dirlewanger could attack with only a few squads at a time. (Author's collection)

and 100 wounded – was running low on ammunition and had to withdraw. The German forces secured the polytechnic by nightfall but halted their attack. German forces did not attack at night in Warsaw.

Realizing that the Germans would soon be close enough to relieve their trapped garrison in PAST, Battalion Kilinski decided to attack the building that night, using information provided by a former Polish employee in PAST. A Polish assault group was able to infiltrate into the basement of the PAST building using an underground passage of which the Germans were unaware. Attacked at close quarters with flame-throwers and grenades, the Germans retreated to the upper floors but once the building caught fire, they were forced to surrender the next morning. During the 20-day siege of the PAST Building, Battalion Kilinski suffered 58 casualties, while the Germans lost 56 killed and 115 captured. The capture of the PAST building was one of the best-planned and executed AK operations of the uprising.

Monter also wanted to remove the German garrison at the Warsaw University complex. In nearby Powisle, Group Krybar had been building an armoured car since 10 August, based on a three-ton Chevrolet truck. They named the armoured car 'Kubus' and it was protected by steel plates and carried one Soviet 7.62mm DP light machine gun, plus a 12-man assault squad. At 0400hrs on 23 August, the Group Krybar used 'Kubus' and a captured German Sdkfz 251 half-track to carry an assault platoon to mount a bold attack on the bunkers at the front entrance of Warsaw University complex. Although the attack was a failure, the Polish armoured attack came as a shock to the Germans, who had become accustomed to machine-gun fire preventing most Polish offensive moves.

The AK troops in Mokotów district were commanded by Podpułkownik Jozef Rokicki (Karol), and these men were not under heavy enemy pressure for much of August. Karol made attempts with Regiment Baszta to break through to Sródmiescie on 13 August and then again on 26 August, but

ATTACK ON WARSAW UNIVERSITY, 23 AUGUST 1944 (pp.76–77)

The German garrison in the grounds of the Warsaw University campus had been a thorn in the side of the AK troops since the beginning of the uprising, but the defences were too strong for the Polish troops to overcome with light weapons. Hauptmann Uhlig had 273 troops from 7. Genesungs Kompanie and one company of the Sicherungs-Bataillon 944, who prevented the Poles in the Powisle district from linking up with the city centre via the Krakowskie Przedmiescie thoroughfare. However, after several earlier failed attempts to storm the university, the AK's Krybar unit in Powisle had begun building an improvised armoured car named 'Kubus' and the unit had also fortuitously captured a German Sdkfz 251 half-track, which was dubbed 'Szary Wilk'. With two armoured vehicles on hand, the commander of Krybar formed an armoured infantry platoon that he intended to use as an assault force for another try against Warsaw University. At 0400hrs on 23 August, the two

Polish vehicles approached the outer defences of the university complex. Under covering fire from an elderly Hotchkiss machine gun (1) mounted in 'Szary Wilk', the assault squad dismounted and threw several Gammon grenades (2) at the university gate. Another Polish soldier attempted to get a PIAT anti-tank (3) launcher into position to knock out the bunker guarding the left side of the gate. Although momentarily surprised by the sudden appearance of Polish armoured vehicles, the German machine gun in the bunker opened fire and mortally wounded the Polish platoon leader, Porucznik Wojciech Brzozowski (Krzysztof) (4). When the remaining assault troops saw Germans attempting to manoeuvre an anti-tank gun into position to engage the two Polish armoured vehicles, they decided to break off the attack and retreated to 'Szary Wilk' and 'Kubus'. Both vehicles were damaged, but able to withdraw.

neither succeeded. Karol was more successful in expanding the AK control to the south and east, moving troops into Sielce, Czerniaków and Sadyba. Battalion Jelen occupied Fort Legionow Dabrowsky, which formed a strong blocking position against German attacks from the south. However, this sector had very few German troops during the early stages of the uprising and Karol was able to establish contact with AK partisan units in the Kabacki Forest, who were able to slip over 400 troops into Sadyba on 18–19 August. It was not until 31 August that Rohr moved against the AK position in Sadyba and a strong attack with artillery and air support rapidly ground down the Polish defence. Fort Legionow was demolished by heavy artillery fire and the Germans occupied Sadyba on 2 September. Polish civilians in this sector were massacred.

THE CITY CENTRE, 3–10 SEPTEMBER

After occupying the Old Town, Bach decided to follow up this success with an effort to reduce the resistance strongholds in the eastern end of Sródmiescie district. Monter's forces held this area in considerable strength and the first German probing attacks launched from the Saxon Gardens on 3 September were easily repulsed. On 5–6 September, Kampfgruppe Reck attacked south from the Saxon Gardens against Polish defences on Krolewska Street, while Dirlewanger's troops tried to breach the main Polish position on Nowy Swiat. The AK troops not only repulsed these German attacks, but mounted several counterattacks that pushed them back to their start lines. Unable to penetrate Monter's defences in Sródmiescie, Bach ordered the Luftwaffe and his artillery to pulverize the district. The area around Napoleon Square was demolished over several days by concentrated Stuka attack and incendiary rockets from the Nebelwerfer in the Saxon Gardens and other areas in the city centre were also set afire. German Stuka attacks concentrated on churches, where Polish civilians were known to be sheltering, deliberately bombing St Alexander's Church and the Holy Cross Church.

A British air-delivery canister in the Warsaw Uprising Museum. A canister like this typically held a single PIAT launcher and six rounds, along with some packaged food, all wrapped in woollen army sweaters. (Author's collection)

Once Powisle was occupied, Bach was finally able to attack the eastern part of Sródmiescie from three directions. German troops firmly occupied the Central Train Station and the Polonia Hotel on Aleje Jerozolimskie and on 7 September these troops began a major attack to seize the critical intersection with Marszalkowska Street, which would effectively cut north–south communications for the insurgents. For two days, the Germans fought over the intersection, attempting to blast open the Polish barricades, but succeeded only in gaining a toehold in the surrounding buildings. Meanwhile, Dirlewanger and Reck attacked the main Polish positions along Nowy Swiat, preceded by concentrated air and artillery attack. After heavy fighting and high losses, the AK troops were finally forced to give ground on 8 September and fall back towards Napoleon Square. At this point, the Germans pressed hard and succeeded in driving a wedge up Warecka Street to within sight of the main post office and Napoleon Square. Virtually the entire area consisted of a mass of shattered, burning ruins. In two more days of fighting, the German troops were able to drive the AK troops out of some of the buildings around Napoleon Square but were unable to recapture the post office. However, the Germans had suffered nearly 5,000 casualties in the first two weeks of September and had barely advanced 300m into the city centre.

THE RED ARMY, 10–14 SEPTEMBER

On 9 September, members of Bór's staff first broached the subject of surrender. It was now apparent that no significant help was on the way to save Warsaw from German retaliation and civilian losses were mounting rapidly. Serious shortages of food, water and ammunition also pointed to the limits of how long the city could endure. At this point, the Germans sensed a flagging in

1 **11 September:** Kampfgruppe Schaper attacks the south end of the insurgent enclave in Czerniaków, capturing part of Lazienkowska Street, but their attack on the port is repulsed.

2 **12 September:** Kampfgruppe Dirlewanger attacks the north side of Czerniaków, focusing on severing the insurgent's link to the city centre by capturing the narrow corridor dominated by the former St Lazarus Hospital and the gasworks.

3 **12 September:** Kampfgruppe Rodewald launches an attack against the west side of Czerniaków, attempting to link up with Dirlewanger's forces on Ksiazeca Street. There is heavy fighting over the large ZUS Building.

4 **1200hrs, 13 September:** as Soviet forces began entering Praga, German pioneers blow up the Poniatowski Bridge.

5 **13 September:** Kampfgruppe Schaper renews the attack on Czerniaków Port with strong artillery support and succeeds in driving Battalion Tur out of this area.

6 **13 September:** Kampfgruppe Dirlewanger captures the former St Lazarus Hospital and the gasworks, while Kampfgruppe Rodewald captures the ZUS Building. The tenuous Polish above ground route from Czerniaków to the city centre is now severed.

7 **14 September:** Radoslaw, the Polish commander in Czerniaków, decides to pull his battered forces back into a tighter perimeter close to the Vistula so that he can establish contact with the Soviet units entering Praga.

8 **15 September:** Radoslaw's forces manage to hold off German attacks on the enclave during the day and to establish contact with the 1st Polish Army (LWP) across the Vistula. By 0430hrs on 16 September, about 300 soldiers under Major Latyshonok from the 3rd Infantry Division have crossed the Vistula River in small boats and joined the AK forces on Solec Street. Their arrival greatly stiffens the insurgent defence in Czerniaków.

9 **16 September:** the Germans demolish an insurgent-held building at the corner of Okrag and Wilanowska streets with a Goliath demolition device, while another German unit captures a Polish military hospital on Zagorna Street and massacres the staff and wounded.

10 **Night, 16 September:** another 900 troops from the LWP 9th Infantry Regiment cross the Vistula River and reinforce the bridgehead in Czerniaków. The LWP forces receive some sporadic artillery support from across the river, but not enough to influence the battle.

11 **19 September:** after several days of fierce fighting against battalions Czata 49 and Broda 53, Dirlewanger's troops occupy much of the length Wilanowska Street. Radoslaw orders his troops to begin evacuating through the sewers to Mokotów. Radoslaw makes it to Mokotów with 200 survivors of his best Kedyw troops, half of whom are wounded.

12 **20 September:** the Germans have installed heavy machine guns to prevent further crossings of the Vistula River. The Soviets do not interfere with this effort or shell these exposed positions.

13 **21 September:** the Polish rearguard under Kapitan Ryszard Bialous (Jerzy) of Battalion Zoska holds only two buildings along the riverfront. However, the Poles and the remaining LWP troops continue to repulse German attacks.

14 **Night, 22 September:** with their ammunition exhausted. Jerzy decides that the survivors will make a breakout. A large group of wounded heads for the wreck of the ship *Bajka* on the Vistula where they hope to cross the river, but they are spotted by the Germans and wiped out by machine-gun and mortar fire. A few survivors succeed in crossing elsewhere. Kapitan Jerzy and four members of Battalion Zoska, wearing their captured SS smocks, succeed in passing themselves off as a German patrol and walk through the enemy lines in the darkness to the city centre. At 0600hrs the next morning, the Germans occupy the rest of the Czerniaków bridgehead and take 140 insurgents captive. The LWP troops are treated as POWs but many of the captured AK troops are shot.

German attack on Czerniaków Bridgehead, 11–23 September 1944

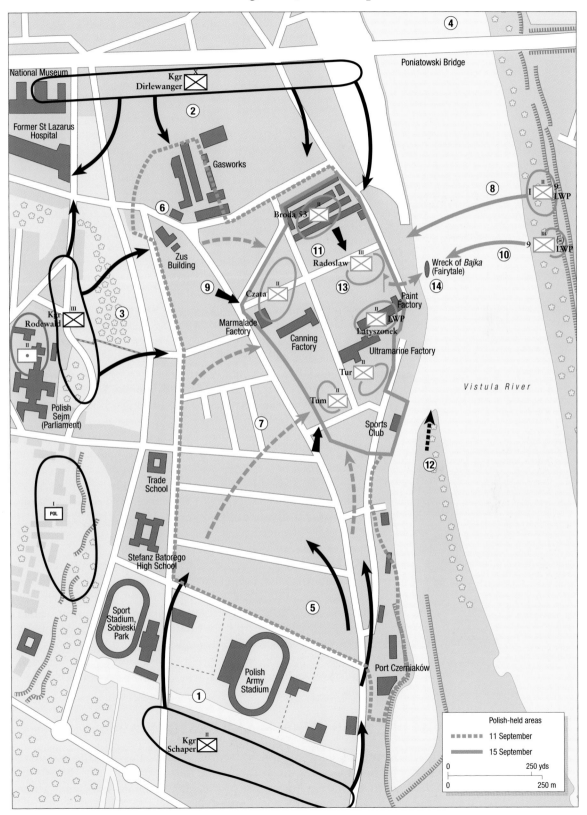

National Museum

Kgr X
Dirlewanger

(4)

Poniatowski Bridge

Former St Lazarus
Hospital

(2)

Gasworks

(6)

Broda 53 II

(8)

I II 9
LWP

(11)
Radosław III

III (=)
9 LWP

(10)

Wreck of *Bajka*
(Fairytale)

(14)

Zus
Building

(9)

Czata II

(13)

Paint
Factory

Kgr III
Rodewald

(3)

Marmalade
Factory

Canning
Factory

Latyszonek II
LWP

Ultramarine Factory

Vistula River

II

Polish
Sejm
(Parliament)

(7)

Tur II

Tum II

Sports
Club

Trade
School

(12)

I
POL

Stefanz Batorego
High School

Sport
Stadium,
Sobieski
Park

(5)

Polish
Army
Stadium

Port Czerniaków

(1)

Kgr II
Schaper

Polish-held areas	
▪▪▪▪▪	11 September
▬▬▬	15 September

0   250 yds

0   250 m

ABOVE LEFT
The Prudential Building burning after being hit by a 600mm mortar shell from 'Ziu' on 28 August 1944. German air and artillery bombardment gradually pulverized this area around Napoleon Square. (Author's collection)

ABOVE RIGHT
A Wehrmacht officer directs the attack near Teatralny Square. Note the cane. (Author's collection)

Polish morale after the loss of the Old Town and the frantic radio broadcasts for help clearly indicated the frustration of the AK's isolation. Generalmajor Rohr sent Bór a letter, suggesting surrender talks to save civilian lives and Bór reluctantly began to consider ending the fight.

Thanks to several GRU agents sent into Warsaw posing as liaison officers, Stalin was quickly apprised of the changing Polish mood. On 10 September, Soviet fighters appeared over Warsaw for the first time since the uprising began and shot down five German aircraft. The next day, Rokossovsky attacked the German IV SS-Panzer Korps, which was defending the eastern bank of the Vistula around Praga. The Soviet 47th Army struck the German 73. Infanterie-Division with three rifle divisions and virtually obliterated this weak formation in two days of fighting. With their thin front collapsing, the German 9. AOK abandoned Praga on 13 September and ordered Pionier-Bataillon 654 to blow up all four bridges over the Vistula River. Soviet troops moved into Praga on 14 September and AK soldiers in Czerniaków could see Soviet troops just across the river.

Since early August, Bór had been trying to establish contact with Rokossovsky by courier and radio, but all attempts had been ignored. Once Soviet troops were only 600m away across the Vistula, a few tentative contacts were made, but the Soviets refused to provide either air or artillery support to the Polish resistance. Still, the arrival of the Red Army brought a halt to talk of surrender. Rokossovsky brought up two of Berling's divisions to secure Praga and to provide the appearance that Polish communist troops were responsible for the liberation of Warsaw. Then Rokossovsky stopped and shifted back to a defensive posture.

ALLIED AIR DROPS, SEPTEMBER 1944

As the uprising dragged into its second month and the appeals of the Polish Government-in-exile became ever more desperate, the British and the Americans grudgingly agreed to provide more support. Two South African and two RAF bomber squadrons joined Polish Flight 1586 in making resupply runs to Warsaw. During the uprising, a total of 199 night sorties were flown from Italy to Warsaw, with 39 aircraft lost (17 Polish, 22 RAF/ SAAF) to deliver about 100 tons of weapons and food. A typical container held 136kg, such as a British 2in. mortar with 20 rounds or a PIAT with eight rounds; two Bren light machine guns with ammunition; 10 rifles or Sten guns; three pistols; four grenades; 100 cans of food preserves and six boxes of biscuits – enough to augment the weaponry of a single AK platoon. Although there is no doubt that the weapons provided – particularly the PIATs – allowed the AK to hold out longer, the RAF delivered only enough equipment to outfit perhaps 15 per cent of the insurgents in Warsaw. In addition to German night fighters and flak, the RAF also had to contend with active Soviet efforts to disrupt the airlift. Not only did the Soviets deny refuelling rights to the RAF, but also a number of Allied aviators noted that their aircraft were repeatedly fired upon by Soviet anti-aircraft and fighters during their supply runs to Warsaw.

Although the Western Allies had requested permission to use Soviet airfields for refuelling after their resupply missions to Warsaw in early August, Stalin did not grant this until 10 September. Since June 1944, Stalin had granted the American Eighth Air Force bombers the use of airfields in the Ukraine in order to conduct 'shuttle-bombing' raids, known as Operation *Frantic*, against German targets in Eastern Europe. After much argument, the government-in-exile was finally able to persuade the Americans to conduct one mission to Warsaw. At 1355hrs on 18 September, the USAAF flew 107 B-17 bombers and 62 P-51 fighters to Warsaw and dropped 1,248 containers. Only one B-17 was lost on the operation. Unfortunately, the area held by the AK was now so small that they could recover only 21 containers. The vast majority landed in German-held territory.

1ST POLISH ARMY (LWP) CROSSING, 15–23 SEPTEMBER

The Polish positions in the Czerniaków district were the closest to the Red Army forces on the Vistula. Although the Germans had not bothered this AK enclave much, this changed as soon as Rokossovsky began his offensive. Bach realized that Czerniaków could provide a valuable bridgehead to facilitate a Soviet crossing of the Vistula and he ordered Dirlewanger to crush it immediately. On 11 September, Dirlewanger's troops moved to sever the thin link between Czerniaków and the city centre – a narrow corridor along Ksiazeca Street. By the next day, Dirlewanger had captured St Lazarus Hospital, cutting off Czerniaków. A Polish attempt to retake the hospital failed.

Inside Czerniaków, the 600 survivors of Group Radoslaw put up a spirited defence, which was bolstered by the appearance of Berling's troops across the river. Radoslaw massed most of his troops in buildings near the river's edge and on 14 September he sent a courier across the river who made contact with the 1st Polish Army (LWP). An officer from the Polish 3rd Infantry Division crossed the river early on 15 September to inform Radoslaw that his unit was going to begin a river-crossing operation that night.

Once darkness fell, a Soviet major led about 300 troops from the 3rd Infantry Division across the Vistula in small boats and landed in Czerniaków. The battalion-sized force brought with it 14 machine guns, 16 anti-tank rifles, five anti-tank guns and eight mortars, which significantly increased Polish firepower in this sector. The LWP troops joined up with Radoslaw's AK troops to defend the key houses along the waterfront, but the rest of the

German attack on Mokotów, 24–27 September 1944

1. 24 September, 1015hrs: 19. Panzer-Division launches a two-battalion attack up Pulawska Street capturing the Krolikarnia Palace. A Polish night counterattack to retake the palace is repulsed.
2. 25 September: German forces continue the attack in southern Mokotów and a vicious battle is fought over a school on Woronicza Street.
3. 25 September: German forces attack the west side of Mokotów and capture the Alkazar redoubt from Battalion Olza.
4. 26 September: German forces advance into the north-west corner of Mokotów.
5. 26 September: Karol orders most of his forces to fall back towards the fortified northern portion of Mokotów. Morale among the defenders and civilians begins to crack. During a brief ceasefire, 9,000 civilians opt to leave the district and march into German custody rather than face further bombardment. At 0400hrs, Karol orders his troops to evacuate to the city centre through the sewers.
6. 26 September: 19. Panzer-Division sends an armour-heavy assault group up Pulawska Street, overrunning several barricades and compressing the Polish forces into a tight area around Karol's headquarters.
7. 27 September, 0800hrs: a strong German attack from several directions commences against the last Polish-held enclave. The remaining Poles surrender at 1200hrs. A total of 2,000 AK fighters and 5,000 civilians march into captivity.

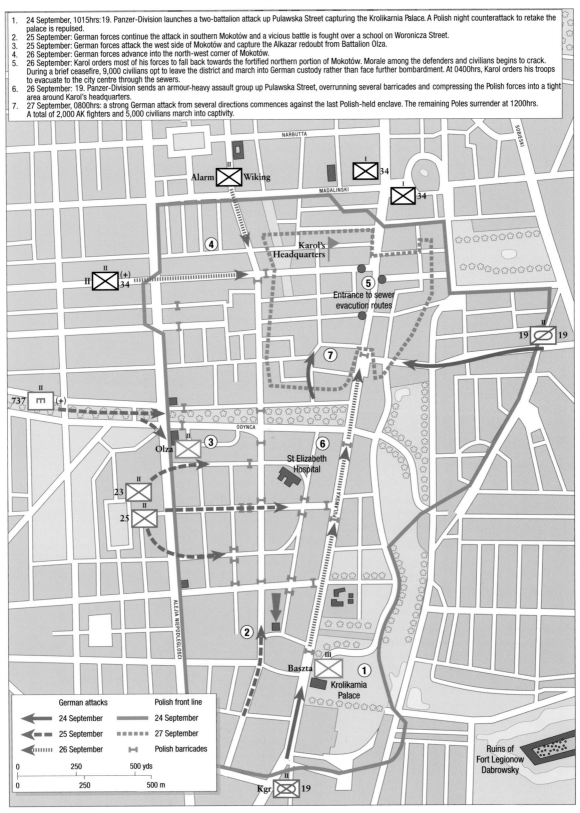

German attacks		Polish front line	
	24 September		24 September
	25 September		27 September
	26 September		Polish barricades

0   250   500 yds

0   250   500 m

German 19. Panzer-Division's attack on Żoliborz, 29–30 September 1944

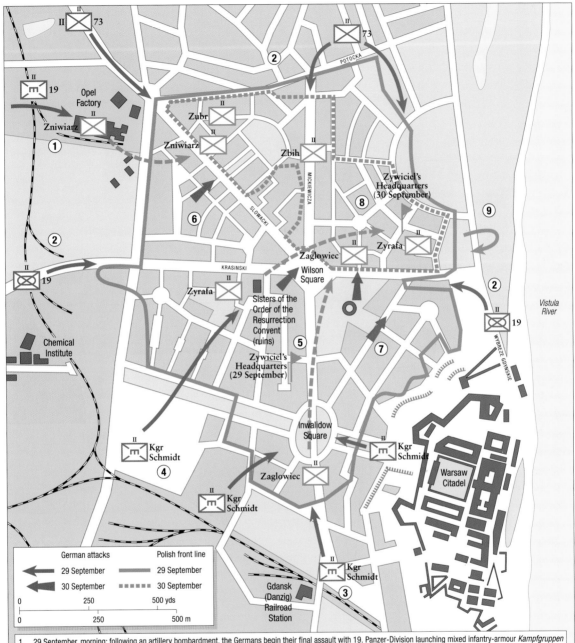

1. 29 September, morning: following an artillery bombardment, the Germans begin their final assault with 19. Panzer-Division launching mixed infantry-armour *Kampfgruppen* against the Polish positions in the Opel Factory and on the west side of Żoliborz. Group Zniwiarz is forced to retreat from the Opel Factory.
2. 29 September, morning: 19. Panzer-Division also launches attacks against the northern, western and eastern sides of Żoliborz, but these gain little ground. The defense by Groups Zbik and Zubr remains firm.
3. 29 September, morning: Kampfgruppe Schmidt launches an attack against Group Zaglowiec from three sides and forces it to retreat toward Inwalidow Square.
4. 29 September: One of Schmidt's assault groups succeeds in penetrating deeply into southeastern Żoliborz and drives Group Zyrafa out of the ruins of the Sisters of the Order of the Resurrection convent.
5. 29 September, evening: Mieczyslaw Niedzielski (Zywiciel), commander of the AK forces in Żoliborz, relocates his headquarters to the north-east side of Wilson Square. Zywiciel, who is severely wounded in the fighting, has established radio contact with Soviet forces across the Vistula. The Soviets promise to assist his AK forces the next day. The AK forces continue to fight for the area south of Krasinski Street.
6. 30 September, dawn: 19. Panzer-Division launches an attack on Slowacki Street that surprises the AK defenders and succeeds in pushing Group Zniwiarz back in disorder.
7. 30 September, morning: Kampfgruppe Schmidt conducts attacks around Wilson Square that succeed in mopping up most of the residual AK resistance south of Krasinski Street. Zywiciel's forces are now compressed into an area measuring barely one kilometre by one kilometre, but Zywiciel expects imminent Soviet intervention.
8. 30 September, 1800hrs: Under orders from Bór, Zywiciel surrenders the final enclave in Żoliborz to 19. Panzer-Division. A total of 1,890 Polish insurgents surrender. For the first time during the uprising, surrendering AK troops are treated as legal combatants by the Germans and not murdered out of hand.
9. 30 September, evening: Zywiciel allows those who are unwilling to trust German guarantees to attempt a breakout toward the Vistula River. Even as the surrender negotiations are in progress, the Soviets continue to promise to provide boats and covering artillery fire. However, the Germans decimate the Polish units trying to escape and only 28 troops swim to the other side. Soviet forces make no effort to assist the breakout whatsoever and no boats are sent to the river.

German StuG III assault guns operating on Foch Street near the Town Hall. German armour had great difficulty in operating inside Warsaw and tended to stay close to the main squares. (Author's collection)

division failed to cross. Most of the Soviet artillery on the east side of the river remained silent and the limited supporting fire was sporadic. Nor did Soviet fighters attempt to counter the German Stukas, which appeared over Czerniaków to bomb the landing sites. On the night of 16 September, Soviet aircraft began dropping weapons, ammunition and food to the enclave in Czerniaków, but since they chose not to use parachutes, much of it was destroyed or damaged on impact. On 17 September, 1,200 more LWP troops crossed the Vistula.

Bach was desperate to crush Czerniaków once the LWP crossings were detected and the combined AK/LWP enclave came under heavy attack. Although Radoslaw put up a very stubborn defence, his forces were quickly worn down by casualties. Schmidt's *Kampfgruppe* pressed down from the north, Dirlewanger from the west and Rohr from the south. Radoslaw's forces were compressed into a four-block area around the paint and canning factories, with German machine gunners controlling access to the riverfront. On 19 September, Radoslaw – who was now wounded – decided to withdraw his remaining 200 troops to Mokotów via the sewers, while a few chose to swim across the Vistula. Kapitan Jerzy repeated his escape from the Old Town by marching his few survivors from Battalion Zoska to Mokotów. A group of Polish wounded and medical personnel who tried to escape across the Vistula were all killed by German gunfire. On the morning of 23 September, Dirlewanger's troops finally occupied Czerniaków, eliminating Berling's bridgehead. SS troops executed over 200 wounded AK troops in the district.

Just as the Czerniaków bridgehead was crumbling, the 1st Polish Army attempted three other small river-crossing operations on the night of 19 September. Several rifle companies from the 3rd Infantry Division attempted to reinforce the Czerniaków landing but were turned back by German mortar and machine-gun fire. The 1st Infantry Division tried to push two rifle battalions across near the new railway bridge, but was also repulsed. Further north, the 2nd Infantry Division managed to get part of a battalion across to link up with some AK holdouts in Marymont, north of Żoliborz, but the Germans crushed this toehold within days. All told, the 1st Polish Army suffered 4,939 casualties in efforts to cross the Vistula, but fewer than 1,500 troops reached the west bank and virtually all who did were killed or captured. Berling himself was relieved of command for 'exceeding his authority' and recalled to Moscow. The fact that Rokossovsky used only a small per cent of his forces in the Warsaw area to mount a river-crossing operation and then failed to provide adequate air or artillery support, demonstrates that this action was little more than a token effort and a sop to the Western Allies.

LAST STANDS IN MOKOTÓW AND ŻOLIBORZ, 23–27 SEPTEMBER

Radoslaw's ever-shrinking band of fighters went from the frying pan into the fire when they arrived in Mokotów. As soon as Czerniaków was finished, Bach shifted strong forces to crush the Poles in Mokotów. Since Rokossovsky's troops had ceased efforts to get across the Vistula, 9. AOK consented to Bach's request for reinforcements and gave him the use of the veteran 19. Panzer-Division and part of Fallschirm-Panzer-Division 1 'Hermann Göring' for a week. On 24 September, the Germans bombarded Mokotów with everything they had and then commenced a two-day attack. The main attack came from the south, with the 19. Panzer committing four Panzergrenadier battalions (with some Panther tanks), a reconnaissance battalion, its pioneers and its self-propelled artillery regiment, as well as some Sturmpanzer IVs. Kampfgruppe Hahn, with a Panzergrenadier battalion from Fallschirm-Panzer-Division 1 'Hermann Göring', a police battalion and two battalions of Cossacks, attacked the north-east corner of Mokotów. Although the AK units under Pułkownik Jozef Rokicki put up a very tough fight, they could not stop well-trained infantry and the 19. Panzer-Division troops

German infantry sprint across Bielanska Street during one of the attacks on Teatralny Square. Dirlewanger's troops were able to gain several footholds near the National Bank, but Polish counterattacks kept throwing them back. (Author's collection)

quickly overran two-thirds of the district. By 25 September, Rokicki's forces were squeezed into a small fortified area and he decided to evacuate his personnel through the sewers to the city centre, which was accomplished over the next two nights. On 27 September, the 19. Panzer-Division occupied the rest of Mokotów. However, unlike the massacres of prisoners that usually followed German advances in Warsaw, Generalmajor Rohr granted POW status to the 2,000 AK troops captured in Mokotów.

In the north, Żoliborz had been one of the quietest sectors for most of the uprising and Polish casualties there had been light. Before tackling Żoliborz itself, Bach ordered three battalions from Fallschirm-Panzer-Division 1 'Hermann Göring', as well as troops from the SS-Panzer-Divisions 'Totenkopf' and 'Wiking', to conduct a sweep of the nearby Kampinos Forest on 27 September. This German sweep killed or drove off the large partisan force that had been operating in the forest since before the uprising and denied the AK troops in Żoliborz a potential escape refuge.

On the morning of 29 September, the Germans launched a major attack upon Żoliborz from the south,

Areas held by the insurgents, 2 October 1944

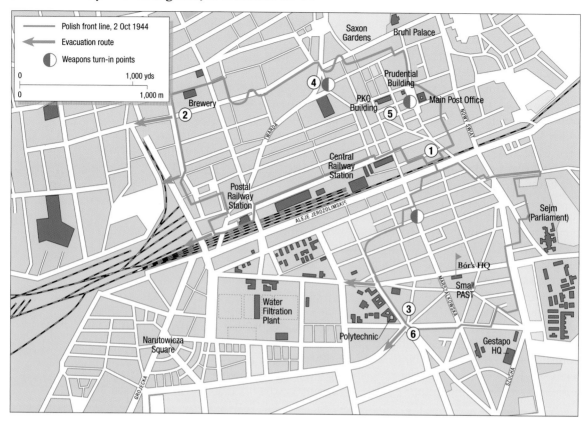

1. 1 October: the Poles still control a barricade that allows communication across the main thoroughfare Aleje Jerozolimskie, connecting both halves of the city centre.
2. 1 October, 0500–1900hrs: some 8,000 Polish civilians evacuate the city centre from five agreed points during a 14-hour truce. Another 16,000 leave the next day but more than 200,000 remain.
3. 2 October, 0800hrs: Bór sends members of his staff to meet with the Germans near the polytechnic, thence to Bach's headquarters, to negotiate the surrender. At 2100hrs, military operations in Warsaw cease. The Germans agree to treat captured AK personnel as legitimate prisoners of war protected by the Geneva Convention. The AK agrees to surrender its personnel on 4–5 October.
4. 4 October, morning: AK units march to three designated points and begin to turn over weapons and ammunition. AK units march into captivity as formed regiments. Most remaining Polish civilians begin leaving Warsaw as well.
5. 4 October, 0940hrs: Radio Lightning makes its last broadcast.
6. 5 October, 0945hrs: the last AK units leave Warsaw. A total of 11,668 Polish soldiers surrender, including Bór and Monter. About 180,000 civilians evacuate the city.

using Kampfgruppe Reck and Kampfgruppe Schmidt, with the 19. Panzer-Division in support. Podpułkownik Zywiciel's 1,500 troops were hard pressed at once – despite the arrival of some anti-tank weapons from the Soviets across the river – and they lost nearly half the district on the first day. The next morning, the Germans launched an attack without the normal artillery preparation and caught the Poles by surprise, capturing several key buildings. Zywiciel established contact with the 1st Polish Army across the river and tried to arrange for an evacuation, but the Soviet advisers failed to provide the necessary boats or artillery support. At this point, orders arrived from Bór to begin negotiations with Bach to surrender the remaining troops in Żoliborz in order to save them from being slaughtered in the final attack. At 1800hrs, the Polish troops in Żoliborz laid down their weapons and they were treated as POWs. One group of AK fighters refused to surrender and made for the river, but only 28 succeeded in reaching Soviet lines.

THE SURRENDER

Once Czerniaków and Mokotów fell, it became obvious to Bór that the Germans now had the strength to crush the resistance quickly in the rest of Warsaw and that neither the Western Allies nor Soviets were going to provide any significant help. Food supplies were exhausted by late September and the civilian population was facing starvation. Although Bór had deferred considering capitulation as long as there was a chance of outside help, that hope was extinguished by the destruction of the Czerniaków bridgehead. Once Bór accepted that capitulation was inevitable, the main issue became to secure the most favourable terms. The two main sticking points were getting the Germans to agree to treat captured AK members as legal POWs and to not harm Warsaw's civilian population.

The only real success achieved by the government-in-exile during the uprising was getting the Anglo-Americans to endorse the concept that AK troops were part of the regular Polish military and thus protected by the 1929 Geneva Convention. Several times during the uprising, Britain publicly broadcast that German soldiers who summarily executed AK soldiers would be held accountable for their crimes. With the end of the war in sight, Bach was willing to be generous to the AK in defeat, in order to speed up the surrender. The fact that Himmler had volunteered to crush an uprising that had gone on for two months was embarrassing to the SS. Without some kind of guarantee that captives would not be handed over to Dirlewanger and his goons, the AK would simply fight to the death. Generalmajor Rohr took a leading role in contacting Bór and it was the guarantees of humane treatment coming from a professional army officer rather than an SS man that enabled the talks to proceed.

On 30 September, Polish emissaries sent to Bach's headquarters were able to gain a German ceasefire on 1 and 2 October in order to evacuate part of Warsaw's civilian population. On 2 October, the Polish delegates signed the capitulation document and all fighting ceased at 2100hrs. In the document, the Germans agreed to treat the AK soldiers as POWs and to deal humanely with Warsaw's population, although it also stipulated that all civilians would be removed from the city. A total of 11,668 AK soldiers formed up into ranks on the morning of 4 October and marched out of Warsaw to surrender; most were sent to POW camps in Germany. Bór and his staff were well treated and sent to Colditz Castle. A few, such as the incredibly resilient Jewish fighters in the ZOB platoon, were able to hide in the ruins and escape later into the forests. Out of about 650,000 civilians who were forcibly evicted from Warsaw, about 20 per cent were sent as forced labour to Germany, 15 per cent were sent to concentration camps and the rest released to become homeless refugees in the Generalgouvernement.

During the 63-day battle for Warsaw, the AK suffered about 15,000 dead or about one-third of its initial force. Civilian casualties are estimated at 200,000 dead, most of whom were murdered by SS troops in the early days of the uprising or killed in the bombardments. About 25 per cent of Warsaw's buildings were destroyed in the fighting. German losses were about 16,000 killed and 9,000 wounded, which works out at a casualty rate of about 50 per cent.

A female soldier in the AK. Initially women were used primarily in support roles, but, as male casualties mounted, women began to appear more and more on the front line. When the AK surrendered, 2,000 female soldiers marched off into captivity. (Author's collection)

AFTERMATH

The city must completely disappear from the surface of the earth and serve only as a transport station for the Wehrmacht. No stone can remain standing. Every building must be razed to its foundation.
Reichsführer Heinrich Himmler, October 17

Once the captured AK soldiers and the civilian population were removed from the city environs, the SS set about the systematic destruction of Warsaw. Hitler's intent was that the city would simply disappear from the face of Europe – the only time in World War II that the Germans actually tried this on a major city. Special German sapper units were sent in to demolish the city with explosives and flame-throwers. By January 1945, the Germans had managed to destroy 85 per cent of Warsaw's buildings and structures.

Aside from the obvious political misjudgements about Allied and Soviet intentions, the AK leaders made a number of critical military mistakes that contributed to their defeat in Warsaw. First, Bór wrecked years of planning for an uprising by attempting to improvise a plan to address a fleeting set of political circumstances, but without taking into account the actual military circumstances. Second, the uprising in Warsaw was not properly coordinated with AK forces outside the capital, so very few reinforcements were received and the Germans were not distracted by multiple rear area threats. Third, the AK failed to target the enemy's centre of gravity, which was communications. If the AK had succeeded in capturing the telephone exchanges on the first day and several of the headquarters, the German response would have been far more sluggish, giving the AK valuable time to organize and receive supplies from the Allies. Tactically, the AK repeatedly failed to mass its forces at key points to seize important positions. However, the AK also demonstrated an incredible tenacity in street fighting that cost the enemy dearly. Despite very limited weapons stockpiles, the AK was able to resist a vastly superior force for 63 days and the Germans never actually destroyed any AK battalions – they just kept slipping away through the sewers to other districts. Ultimately, the AK was not able to make the transition from a decentralized guerrilla force to a centrally directed light infantry force because of a lack of adequate communications equipment, training and prior planning. Essentially, the fight was conducted by sector commanders with minimal central planning or control – at few points in the battle was the AK leadership able to use its reserves to mount major attacks or to deal with German breakthroughs. This inability to transform into a more cohesive, organized army forced the AK to fight a piecemeal battle that ceded the initiative to the Germans.

The Germans also made a number of critical mistakes that caused the fighting to drag on, beginning with their failure to interdict fully the sewer systems. Time and again, AK forces used the sewers to escape German encirclements and without them, AK losses would have been much heavier

early in the battle. Bach and Reinefarth also failed to appreciate the value of denying water and electricity to the city until well into the campaign. German atrocities committed against civilians stiffened the opposition and helped to resign the civilian population to enduring widespread suffering much longer than would otherwise have occurred. It must also be pointed out that the Germans were able to suppress the Warsaw Uprising only because of the protracted Soviet inactivity on the 9. AOK front outside Warsaw and the unwillingness of the Allies to provide the AK with significant amounts of weaponry. Overall, both sides fought with a level of incompetence that nullified many of their intrinsic advantages and contributed to the development of a brutal, attritional slug-fest.

On 12 January 1945, the Soviets began the long-awaited Vistula–Oder Offensive and five days later, the 1st Polish Army marched into the ruins of Warsaw. Once the war ended four months later, the Soviets rapidly set about constructing a puppet regime in Poland, although for a brief period they allowed the façade of cooperation with non-communist elements. Prime Minister Mikolajczyk returned to Poland and, together with AK veterans, tried to stem the inevitable communist takeover. Despite Stalin's promises to the Western Allies at Yalta in February 1945 to allow free elections in Poland, the communists rigged the elections in 1947, effectively creating a one-party state. The communists then used their secret police to hunt down all opponents and either murder, imprison or force them into exile. Marshal Rokossovsky was appointed Polish Minister of Defence. The new communist overlords excised all references to the Warsaw Uprising and the massacre at Katyn Forest.

Most of Warsaw lay in ruins after the two-month battle and the Germans demolished what remained. (Nik Cornish)

In England, the government-in-exile and the 195,000 Polish regular military personnel quickly found themselves in limbo, once the United States and Britain recognized the new communist government in Warsaw in July 1945. After being released from prison in Germany, Bór settled in Britain and became Prime Minister of the government-in-exile from 1947 to 1949. The Western Allies further betrayed Poland by failing to indict either Bach or Reinefarth at the post-war Nuremberg Trials. Although the Polish military forces in the West were disbanded after the war, the government-in-exile maintained a shadowy existence for the next four decades, recognized only by the Vatican, Spain and Ireland. It seemed that this relic of a lost cause served no purpose and had no future. Yet the Poles are a stubborn lot and this proved to be their national salvation. Despite utter defeat at the hands of the Nazis and communists in 1944–45, the government-in-exile refused to accept defeat and continued to appoint new Prime Ministers for more than 40 years. In 1991, the last Prime Minister of the government-in-exile, Ryszard Kaczorowski, returned to Poland and handed the pre-war presidential seals and other documents preserved from Nazi and communist occupation to Lech Walesa, the first president of post-communist Poland. Today, the Third Reich and the Soviet Union lie in the dustbin of history, and Poland once again is a free and independent republic. The AK has been rehabilitated and its heroes honoured, while the Stalinist stooges have been consigned to well-deserved obscurity. Thus, the sacrifices of 1944 were – in the long run – worth it.

Modern historiography tends to depict the Warsaw Uprising as a militarily doomed and tragic exercise, which has elements of truth in it. However, these analyses fail to connect the intensity of Polish national resistance in 1944 with its influence upon the Soviet occupation from 1945 to 1991. After the doomed fight in Warsaw, the Soviets knew that the Poles would fight again if pressed too hard and this was demonstrated by the Poznan riots in 1956. Rokossovsky, who had refused to use his tanks to help Warsaw in 1944 used them in 1956 to suppress Polish workers, which provoked a firestorm of protest. In short order, Polish communists packed Rokossovsky off to Moscow and took measures to pacify the nationalistic outburst. It reappeared 14 years later with the emergence of the Solidarity Trade Union. Although the Soviets prepared a military invasion to suppress the nationalism unleashed by Solidarity, the memory of the Warsaw Uprising gave them pause. By this time, the geriatric leadership in the Kremlin had little stomach for a bloodbath in Poland and they opted to use the Polish communist regime to suppress Solidarity with martial law. Instead, Solidarity emerged from this period of repression stronger than ever, which led to the collapse of communism in Poland and the weakening of the entire Soviet Empire.

THE BATTLEFIELD TODAY

A reconstruction of the 'Kubus' armoured car at the Polish Museum in Warsaw. The actual 'Kubus' is parked at the back of the Warsaw Uprising Museum. (Author's collection)

Although the city of Warsaw was virtually obliterated by the end of 1944, there is much to see in the modern reincarnation of the Polish capital that is relevant to the Warsaw Uprising. Front and centre in this effort to shed light on their wartime resistance is the Warsaw Uprising Museum at 79 Grzybowska Street in Wola, which opened in 2004. This is a very modern, well-put-together museum. Virtually all displays have legends in both Polish and English, and the museum shop offers an excellent guidebook in English, French, German and Russian. The first floor of the museum has a full-size replica of one of the B-24 Liberator bombers that flew resupply missions to Warsaw. The museum has a total of 47 displays on three levels. There are also two cinemas showing period films, with subtitles in English. Outside the museum, there is a vast wall with the names of the dead inscribed, as well as the original 'Kubus' armoured car and a German concrete bunker.

The other major museum in Warsaw that has significant coverage on the uprising is the Polish Army Museum at 3 Aleje Jerozolimskie. This collection is housed in a wing of the Polish National Museum and the Ministry of Defence runs it. A large collection of armoured vehicles, aircraft and artillery is located outside the museum, including an Sdkfz 251 half-track, a Hetzer tank destroyer, some German artillery from 1944, an 800mm shell from 'Dora' and the 600mm shell from 'Ziu'. Inside the museum, which covers Polish military history from the medieval to the modern eras, the exhibits on the Uprising are located on the second floor and include excellent displays on uniforms and weapons. Unfortunately, this is not a very user-friendly museum: photography was not allowed inside the building, nor were there English-language guidebooks or translations for any of the exhibits. Another smaller museum of note is the Gestapo Museum at 25 Szucha, which is located inside the courtyard of the Ministry of Education.

Walking through Warsaw's Old Town, which has been completely restored to its pre-war configuration, it is easy to see how even poorly-armed defenders could hold off a modern army for so long. Streets such as Piwna are only three metres wide and four-storey buildings tower over anyone standing on the cobblestones below. Even the numerous churches in the area are so stoutly built, with thick concrete or brick walls, that it is clear that the entire area could be converted into a fortress. Throughout both the Old Town and the New Town, there are numerous monuments and plaques dedicated to the uprising, including the large Warsaw Uprising Monument on Dluga Street, next to the former Krasinski Palace. Many of the AK battalions have plaques noting their accomplishments and their casualties.

BIBLIOGRAPHY

Primary sources
German Records at NARA: 9. AOK.

Secondary sources
Abramian, Eduard, *Forgotten Legion: Sonderverbände Bergmann in World War II 1941–1945* Bayside, NY: Europa Books Inc., 2007

Bór-Komorowski, T., *The Secret Army* Nashville, TN: the Battery Press, 1984

Borodziej, Wlodzimierz, *The Warsaw Uprising of 1944* Madison, WI: University of Wisconsin Press, 2001

Borowiec, Andrew, *Destroy Warsaw! Hitler's Punishment, Stalin's Revenge* Westport, CT: Praeger Publishers, 2001

Davies, Norman, *Rising '44: the Battle for Warsaw* London: Penguin Books, 2003

Deschner, Gunther, *Warsaw Rising* New York: Ballantine Books, 1972

Garlinski, Jozef, *Poland, S.O.E. and the Allies* London: George Allen & Unwin Ltd, 1969

Harrison, E. D. R., 'The British Special Operations Executive and Poland', *The Historical Journal*, Vol. 43, No. 4 (Dec. 2000), pp. 1071–91

Kirchmayer, Jerzy, *Powstanie warszawskie* Warsaw: Książka i Wiedza, 1959

Ney-Krwawicz, Marek, *The Polish Home Army 1939–45* London: Polish Underground Movement Study Trust, 2001

Likiernik, Stanislaw, *By Devil's Luck: A Tale of Resistance in Wartime Warsaw* Edinburgh: Mainstream Publishing Company, 2001

Lukas, Richard C., *Forgotten Holocaust: the Poles under German Occupation 1939–1944* New York: Hippocrene Books, 1997

MacLean, French L., *The Cruel Hunters: SS-Sonderkommando Dirlewanger* Atglen, PA: Schiffer Publishing, 1998

Radzievsky, Alexei I., *Tankovyi Udar: Tankovay armiii v nastupatelnoy operaqii fronta po opytu velikoi otecestvennoy voiny* [*Tank Attack: The Tank Army in Offensive Operations as Experienced in the Great Patriotic War*] Moscow: Voenizdat, 1977

Rozwadowski, Piotr, *Wojsko Powstania Warszawskiego, Warszawskie Termopile 1944* Warsaw: Ministry of National Defense, 2006

Ulankiewicz, Andrzej Rafal, '*Warski II*'. *Wawelska Street Redoubt* unpublished manuscript

Zawodny, Janusz K., *Nothing But Honor: the Story of the Warsaw Uprising 1944* Stanford: Stanford University Press, 1979

Websites
There are a large number of very detailed websites providing a wealth of information about the Warsaw Uprising.

http://powstanie-warszawskie-1944.ac.pl/

Excellent website in Polish focuses on the organization and operations of the AK.

http://wilk.wpk.p.lodz.pl/~whatfor/niemcy_w_powstaniu1.htm

Excellent website in Polish on the German order of battle during the Warsaw Uprising.

http://www.1944.pl/

This is the official website of the Warsaw Rising Museum, offering a great deal of information in English, Polish, French, German and Russian.

http://www.warsawuprising.com/

Another excellent website in English, which provides a large number of eyewitness accounts from both sides, photographs and other resources.